Think It Strong

Transforming Your Marriage/Relationship by The Power of Your Thoughts

Written By:

Rachel Kalukango-Harris, MSW
Ronald Harris Jr.

ACKNOWLEDGMENTS

This journey began for us many years ago as God began to challenge our thoughts and challenge our beliefs. For so long, we lived a limited life while God was calling us to experience an abundant life in Him. We desired this abundant life, but we were not sure how to move our lives forward in a way that would create and support this abundance that we desired. Over time, God began to renew our minds in a way that pushed us towards creating and embracing a limitless life. This change happened gradually, and it all began with the renewing of our minds. As God began to make us aware of the limiting thoughts that polluted our minds, we began to do the work to change all that we did not desire to have in our lives. That journey has finally led us to the creation of this book. We wrote this book with the hope and belief that those that shall read it and work to renew their minds will not only experience abundance in their marriage or relationship but also in their lives. We would first like to say thank you to God who continues to renew our thoughts, minds, and hearts along this path of life. Thank you to our four beautiful boys Ronald III, Rashad, Ryan, and Ryder who have made this life a breath of fresh air. We are grateful to have co-created you with God and can't wait to see all that your thoughts create for your own lives. Thank you to our parents that raised and created two evolving human beings. Thank you to the countless friends and family that support us and our union. Thank you to the *Married by God family of supporters* that allowed us to pour into you all that God pours into us. We are forever grateful for your love and support.

FOREWORD

"As a man thinks in his heart, so is he".
"Whether you think you can, or you think you can't, you are right".
"Inward thoughts create outward realities."

Each of the statements above centers on the same powerful truth, the life that we live is driven by the thoughts that we think. The difference between a good outcome and a bad outcome in any experience is the way in which you choose to see it. The same is true for marriage. The foundation of a good relationship isn't the actions that you put in it, but the thoughts that you think towards it. If you think your union is strong, no matter what comes at it, what you go through, or what particular misunderstanding that may arise, the outcome will always be good because you "think it to be".

As a follow up to their initial writing "The Blueprint", the Harris' look to make an in-depth exploration of this master key of thought, and offer up tools to help couples enhance and better their unions. As you read this book and apply the principles contained within to your life, you can expect a definite change for the better. You will learn how to identify the thoughts you think, control what you choose to focus on and recognize how your own thought life has contributed to what you are currently experiencing in your marriage or relationship. Having taken the time to apply these timeless principles to my own life and relationship, I can attest to the fact that no matter how you feel about your spouse, once you finish this reading, that feeling together with your experiences will be elevated to a higher and more intense level of love, understanding, and intimacy. This will not be the result of you getting more money, although you may find that the use of these principles may cause you to make a career change. It won't be the result of you having a better sex life, although you may find your intimacy increasing in and out of the bedroom. It won't be the result of your spouse doing what you have always wanted them to do, although you may see a change in behavior. No, while all these aforementioned factors may play a part in your perception that things have improved, the ultimate reason will be because you chose to "THINK IT STRONG".

Godspeed – Dr. Sean Cook D.C.C TH. D
N.C.C.A Licensed Christian Counselor

Think It Strong: Transforming Your Marriage or Relationship by the Power of Your Thoughts
Published by MARRIED BY GOD, LLC
ATLANTA, GEORGIA, U.S.A.

Copyright ©2019 Rachel Kalukango-Harris, MSW and Ronald Harris Jr. All rights reserved.

No part of this book may be reproduced in any form or by any mechanical means, including information storage and retrieval systems without permission in writing from the publisher/author, except by a reviewer who may quote passages in a review.

All images, logos, quotes, and trademarks included in this book are subject to use according to trademark and copyright laws of the United States of America.

KALUKANGO-HARRIS, RACHEL, and HARRIS, RONALD JR., Authors
THINK IT STRONG
Rachel Kalukango-Harris, MSW and Ronald Harris Jr.

ISBN: **13: 978-1-7338658-0-7**

FAMILY & RELATIONSHIPS / Marriage & Long-Term Relationships

QUANTITY PURCHASES: Schools, churches, companies, professional groups, clubs, and other organizations may qualify for special terms when ordering quantities of this title. For information, email marriedbygod2015@gmail.com.

All rights reserved by Rachel Kalukango-Harris, MSW, Ronald Harris Jr.,
and Married By God, LLC.
This book is printed in the United States of America.

Contents

Introduction i

Chapter One: Godly Thoughts 1

Chapter Two: Thoughts from the Enemy 7

Chapter Three: Thoughts from Others 13

Chapter Four: Our Thoughts 21

Chapter Five: Control Your Thoughts 27

Chapter Six: Believing in Blessed 33

Chapter Seven: Alignment- My Priority is God's Priority 37

Chapter Eight: The Mental Choice-To Live or Die 43

Chapter Nine: You Have Not Because You Ask Not 47

Chapter Ten: God's Wisdom Vs. Your Wisdom 53

Chapter Eleven: Giving Is Tied to Receiving 57

Chapter Twelve: Will Your Thoughts 61

Chapter Thirteen: Your Marriage/Relationship Is Your Creation 65

Chapter Fourteen: Fear, the Silent Killer to Manifestation 71

Chapter Fifteen: Focus on The Good Until Good Is All You See 77

Chapter Sixteen: Abundant Life in Marriage/Relationships 81

Chapter Seventeen: Think Like One, Act Like One, Build Like Two 87

Chapter Eighteen: No Limits 91

Introduction

Everything that was ever anything began with a thought. From the beginning, when God formed the world, He had already had a thought of what it would be and simply created it. God's ability to think a thing and speak it into existence has been the great mystery of all believers and non-believers on earth. Our very being stems from God's thoughts about creating man in His image and likeness. What a tremendous gift from the Almighty to be made in His image and likeness. Think about it; if we are made of God, created to be like God, then surely, we have the powers that God exhibits throughout His word. Perhaps, the ability to fully utilize our thoughts to shape and create our realities hasn't been fully explored or realized by many of us. The image and likeness of God, therefore, must not only exist in the physical resemblance of God but must also be reflected in the mental and creational ability of God within us.

As early as I can recall, thoughts have always been a part of my life. Before I could communicate verbally, thoughts were floating in my mind without the ability to effectively articulate them. This is true for all infants prior to learning how to speak. God has shaped each of us to think or envision things for ourselves before they ever exist physically. In the infancy of our lives, most of our thoughts are innocent and pure. As children, our thoughts are as free as birds with no cage to contain or restrict their possibilities. We tend to believe that we will experience the best out of life and all that it has to offer. As we age and experience more of life, our thoughts begin to become weighed down and influenced by the world we live in, negative experiences we encounter, and what we begin to believe about ourselves. Our thoughts are guided by the way we choose to see and feel about things that affect and impact our lives. With thoughts being so fragile and important to our lives, it's clear why the Bible says in *Proverbs 23:7*, *"For as he thinks within his heart, so is he".* **Simply meaning that whatever you think to be true and real about yourself, your situation, or others will be evident in your behavior, thus in your life**. For example, I believe that my husband loves me unconditionally (agape love). I believe it so deeply that no one can persuade me to feel any differently about it. The belief that I have about my husband and my marriage show in my daily actions towards him. I'm loving, respectful and encouraging of him because deep down, I know he loves me as well. Even in his faults, I can say love is wrapped within it. My thoughts about the love my husband has for me, directly impact my marriage and drive the actions I show towards him to be positive and full of love.

Just like thoughts can have a positive effect, they can also have a negative effect on our marriage/relationship. Norman Vincent Peale once said, "If you think in negative terms you will achieve negative results, but if you think in positive terms you will obtain positive results." Many years ago, I can recall dating a guy that was no good for me. He treated me decent but, in my heart, I knew he was cheating and was a liar. I realize that my actions towards him showed what I really felt in my heart about him. I was dismissive of him, secretive with him and withheld my love because I didn't trust him. The thoughts I had about him shaped who I was with him negatively because my thoughts about him were negative. But be careful not to confuse thoughts with facts. Facts are not thoughts. Facts are facts. **Facts don't necessarily impact our marriage or relationships. The thoughts we have about the facts are what impact our marriage/relationship.** For instance, if someone is unfaithful in the marriage or relationship, we can choose to think that they made a mistake and are truly sorry for the discretion, so we move towards forgiveness and reconciliation with them. The FACT remains that they were unfaithful. On the other hand, we can think they are not sorry for cheating and will cheat again, which will prevent any chance of reconciling and repairing the marriage or relationship. **Our thoughts are the pendulum between success and failure in our marriage or relationship.** While we are not always able to control our thoughts, we do have the ability to determine what we do with them and how they affect our lives.

It would be remiss of us to prepare you to control your thoughts without first discussing who gives the power to control thoughts. There is no way to have full control over your thoughts or your life without first having a relationship with God and knowing who you are in Him. God grants us all the knowledge and wisdom to control our thoughts and therefore, control our actions. God's word is a lamp unto our feet which guides us in living a life full of joy and peace even while experiencing hardships and trials. Therefore, before you begin, review *Matthew 6:33, "Seek the Kingdom of God above all else, and live righteously, and He will give you everything you need".* Once you begin to seek God, everything you need to think and live abundantly and experience a prosperous marriage or relationship will be given to you, but you must make the choice to receive it.

We have learned that in life, we may not always be able to control what happens to us. There are times when tragedy strikes us all, and we are faced with obstacles and hardships that we did not ask for. In those times, our perspective (thought) about it typically drives the level of positive or negative impact it has on our lives. Some people face tough times and fold under pressure while others give it their all and overcome what had the potential to destroy them. When something negative happens to us, we can't change the fact that it happened, but we can change the type of impact it has on us. We can determine if this experience will influence us positively or negatively.

Research shows that we all have thousands of thoughts a day. Some of you are thinking it would be impossible to control all the thoughts I have daily, but we beg to differ. Luckily for you, we are focusing on simply controlling those thoughts that would impact your marriage or relationship. If we are honest with ourselves, all of us dream of having a wonderful marriage or relationship. We typically don't wish to meet and date someone that we will be miserable with, and we surely don't hope to marry someone that will make us miserable and unhappy for the rest of our lives. Most times, the thoughts we have when we initially get married or start a committed relationship are joyous, happy, and hopeful of the future life we may share with our spouse or significant other. If this is the case, how do some people begin down a path of hateful, disgusted, and negative feelings about their significant other or spouse? When do the feelings of love turn to feelings of hate in a relationship? Our belief is that this transition is gradual. It is not something that happens immediately for most people. It is a slow, sneaky progression guided by a shift in thoughts. **Your thoughts can either feed and heal your marriage/relationship or poison and starve it to death.** When we fail to pay attention to what our thoughts are and simply deposit them into our hearts, we are unaware of what we are putting into our marriage/relationship. The Word of God says, *"Watch over your heart with all diligence, for from it flow the springs of life," Proverbs 4:23.* Here, we must understand the connection of Proverbs 23:7 and Proverbs 4:23. We must guard our hearts diligently because what we think in our heart is what we become and experience in the world. There is no way to guard your heart without first guarding the thoughts that take residence in your heart.

Our goal for those who read this book is that God will begin to transform your mind in a way that allows you to focus on every thought you have about your marriage/relationship, and begin to assess its value or detriment if accepted in your heart. We believe that this book will assist in renewing your mind to experience the abundance that God has for us all. We believe that by utilizing the skills we teach in this book, your thoughts will not only begin to become more positive, purposeful, and God-like, but the overall state of your marriage/relationship will begin to shift positively because you have now transformed your thoughts to positively transform your marriage/relationship. Your thoughts have 'creation' power in your life. Whatever you think and believe is what you create in the experiences that you have in life. You are a co-creator with God. We hope that this book will awaken the God within you to truly understand the power that God has given us all to shape our lives.

Chapter One
Godly Thoughts

I have always wondered where thoughts originate from. Perhaps, every thought stems from a place, an encounter, a past memory, a current event, or a desire we may have. Life has placed many thoughts along my mental path that have helped me but also hindered me along this journey of life. This may be true for you as well. Over time, God has come to reveal that thoughts originate from four main places in our lives. Our thoughts can originate from the Almighty God, the ever so cunning enemy (devil), from ourselves, and from others. These inspired thoughts can affect what we think about ourselves, our relationships, our circumstances, and our future. When we understand where the thoughts we have originate from, we can determine the impact they will have on our lives and relationships if we deposit them in our hearts.

The most powerful thought you can ever have in your life is a godly thought. A godly thought is a thought generated by aligning your spirit with God's and His word. **Godly thoughts are the only thoughts that should always be deposited into your heart. Godly thoughts never have to be assessed or measured of their worthiness or goodness in your life, for they are designed to prosper your life.** Godly thoughts are thoughts that uplift, encourage, bring peace, power, purpose, victory, blessings, and truth in your life and in your marriage/relationship. Remember, for a godly thought to transform your marriage/relationship, you must first seek and continuously build your relationship with God. When you have a relationship with God, godly thoughts naturally come to your mind. Through prayer and studying of God's Word, you begin to release godly thoughts into your life. For instance, there are times I may feel discouraged, and I go to read God's Word for some encouragement. In my mind, I believe that reading God's Word will encourage me, but it has an even deeper effect than what I sought out from it. While only looking for encouragement, God's Word feeds me thoughts of victory and power over the very issue that I felt discouraged about. Believe me, if you haven't experienced it, the power of godly thoughts can totally transform your mind and emotions.

Some people believe that godly thoughts must be wrapped in religious jargon or sound so spiritual that they miss the simplicity that is a godly thought. For instance, the Bible says in *Matthew 21:22*, *"And whatever you ask in prayer, you will receive, if you have faith".* There is nothing simpler than understanding this verse and using it to fuel your thoughts around your marriage/relationship. Here, the Word of God is simply revealing to us that if you take the time to pray and talk to God, whatever you ask Him while doing so in prayer or talking to God, you will receive. Now, receiving is not just a possibility. Receiving is a guarantee when you pray and talk to God about it, believing it is done as you pray. **So, if your thoughts about**

God changing a situation in your marriage/relationship are positive and full of faith, God can release that change in your life because you have the faith and positive thought to receive it. There is no way to have faith without having godly thoughts. Godly thoughts help to support, build and protect our faith in God. Godly thoughts are wrapped in positivity and hope. His Word says, *"For I know the plans I have for you," says the LORD. "They are plans for good and not for disaster, to give you a future and a hope" (Jeremiah 29:11).* If God's plans for us are for us to experience good things, then why do we attach negative thoughts to our godly life? We will look more into this as we discuss the enemy's thoughts in the next section. Here, I want you to truly understand the power that godly thoughts have in transforming the way you see, feel, and experience your marriage/relationship.

I can recall early in my marriage, around year three, when I began to have some negative thoughts about my marriage and husband. I began to feel overwhelmed and unsupported in the marriage. These were the thoughts that ran through my head. As a working wife, a grad student, a mother of two boys and expecting a third child, I was frustrated with my marriage. There were times I felt like I was doing all I could for the marriage and to help, but here we were still struggling financially to get on our feet. If I am honest, I began to have thoughts about my husband like, "He wasn't doing enough", "he needs to get a second and even third job", and "he doesn't really care about us doing well". I know that the enemy and what I fed myself began to implant negative thoughts into me about my marriage and my husband. When I prayed at night to God to change our circumstances and help me to not feel this way about my husband, God reminded me of all the good that my husband brought to our marriage. He reminded me that my husband worked very hard for our family. He had a job where he worked overtime many nights as well as a small business that supplied extra money to our home. He was a great father helping the kids with homework and getting them ready for bed or picking them up from school. When I needed time to study or write papers for school, he made sure the kids were taken care of and would even drive me every other weekend in the summer from Atlanta to Valdosta, to go to class which was about a three-and-a-half-hour one-way drive. Not only that, he was an attentive husband, loving me and showing me affection even when I didn't always show it back. In that moment with God, He began to remind me of all the positive thoughts I had about my husband that I let become overshadowed by the negative thoughts in my mind. It happens to us all. We experience a trial or rough time in our marriage/relationship, and we begin to focus on all that is wrong within it. We begin to magnify the negative thoughts instead of magnifying God in our life who can magnify the godly thoughts we need. **Godly thoughts in a marriage remind us of the humanness of our spouse, significant other and ourselves.** They remind us that even the terrible things in our lives and marriage/relationships, all work together for our good in God. God's Word says, *"All things work together for the good of them that love the Lord and who are called according to His purpose" Romans 8:28.* Placing your marriage/relationship in God will always have you experiencing the good of life even when hit with bad moments, which we all may face. You will be able to see a better marriage or a better relationship because your thoughts feed you with God's Word and power in your life. **When God is in your marriage/relationship, its success and well-being become part of God's purpose.** God is known to care for and protect things that belong to Him and are dear to Him. When you take God out of your marriage, you take away the ability to make all things work for your good and the ability to see it as so. You kill the possibility of positivity in the outlook of your marriage/relationship. Positive thoughts are always aligned with God. The Word of God says, *"I come that you might have life and have it more abundantly."* All abundant life is wrapped in joy and love. There is no way to truly experience abundant life without love, for God is love. When your thoughts begin to shape your marriage or relationship to experience an abundant life, you are now controlling your thoughts and making them work for your good. **Remember, abundant life doesn't begin with having abundant things. Instead, it begins with having abundant thoughts full of positivity shaped by godly thoughts.**

Majority of happy and blessed marriages or relationships that you see have godly thoughts running rampant throughout them. They have mastered the ability to guard their minds in a way that generates godly thoughts and deposits them into their heart. **When godly thoughts enter your heart, they have the ability to transform your life.** They can transform the way you see your spouse/significant other from negative to positive, thus having the power and ability to transform your actions towards them, and eventually transforming your marriage or relationship. Remember, godly thoughts are higher than the thoughts we could ever have. The Word of God says in *Isaiah 55:8, "My thoughts are nothing like your thoughts," says the LORD, "And my ways are far beyond anything you could imagine."* We must understand that if God holds the ultimate knowledge and wisdom in His thoughts, then we must begin to have godly thoughts so that we may tap into its power in our marriage/relationship. For instance, you may be someone who has a very negative outlook on life. You wake up feeling the day will go wrong before your feet even touch the floor. You may never think well of your spouse and find yourself just existing in the marriage with your negative thoughts. The enemy is trying to convince you that this is just the way you are and that you don't have the power to change it. Do not conform to this mindset or believe it. God's Word has a godly thought waiting to feed your spirit and your mind. A godly thought to counter such thoughts are, *"I can do all things through Christ who strengthens me", Philippians 4:13.* That means you have the power to transform your negative thoughts into godly thoughts. You don't have to be able to do it on your strength. All you need to do is seek and acknowledge God and tap into His strength. When you tap into the strength of God, you tap into His thoughts, for in His thoughts lie His strength. No more self-destructive thoughts about your marriage or your relationship. Align the thoughts about your husband, wife, or significant other with godly thoughts.

Godly thoughts are the only thoughts that can reboot, refuel, and refocus a dying marriage or relationship. When you begin to allow godly thoughts in your mind and heart, they begin to transform the way you see yourself in the marriage/relationship and the way you see the situations that you face. **Godly thoughts have the power to produce godly words, which produce godly actions, which can transform our marriage/relationship into joyfully blessed ones.** The Word of God is full of thoughts that you can and should be using daily in your marriage/relationship. God has given us all the ability to choose our thoughts. Stop believing that you have no control over the thoughts you have or the feelings you feel. You are made in the image of God which releases power in you when connected to God. Decide today to begin to feed yourself Godly thoughts about yourself and your marriage/relationship. Spend more time focusing on the positive aspects of your marriage/relationship instead of zooming in on the negative. If you fill your head and heart with godly thoughts, it will begin to manifest in your life and in your marriage/relationship.

As believers, we must spend the majority of our time, consuming information and influence that will generate godly thoughts in our minds and hearts. We must be careful not to spend so much time being fed from the influences of the world especially when it comes to our marriage/relationship. So many television shows promote infidelity, selfishness, and greed in marriage and relationships, that many of them are not lasting and thriving anymore. In Philippians 4:8, Paul teaches us what things we should spend our time focusing on that can impact our lives. He says, *"And now, dear brothers and sisters, one final thing. Fix your thoughts on what is true, and honorable, and right, and pure, and lovely, and admirable. Think about things that are excellent and worthy of praise."* Everything that God teaches us is true, for He is the true living God. When you go to God to generate thoughts, what He gives you will fit exactly what Paul is talking about in this scripture. Take your marriage/relationship and think about what is true, honorable, right, pure, lovely and admirable about it. Don't let the enemy convince you that it doesn't exist in your marriage or relationship when God has shown you proof that it does. Remember, your ability to generate godly thoughts will only be as powerful as your relationship is with Him. Spend time daily consulting with God about your marriage or relationship. Ask Him to guide your thoughts and actions throughout the day towards your spouse or significant other. God can do exceedingly and abundantly far more than we could ever ask or think, so allow God to shift your marriage/relationship by transforming your current thoughts into godly ones.

As stated earlier, the only way to begin to have godly thoughts is to tap into the spirit of God. The Holy Spirit is the spirit of God within us. He is the translator between Gods thoughts and our understanding. There is no way to generate godly thoughts without a godly spirit working within you. In *1 Corinthians 2:11 it states, "For who knows a person's thoughts except their own spirit within them. In the same way no one knows the thoughts of God except the Spirit of God".* The Holy Spirit allows us to generate godly thoughts within ourselves that can feed our marriage or relationship. The Spirit of God is the only connection that streams and downloads godly thoughts into us to utilize. That's why it is important to understand and cultivate the fruits of the Spirit in your life and marriage/relationship. When you are tapped into the Spirit of God, and godly thoughts are being deposited into your marriage/relationship, you will begin to see and feel love, joy, peace, patience, kindness, goodness, faithfulness, gentleness, and self-control in your marriage/relationship, which are the fruits of the Spirit found in Galatians 5:22-23. This is an area where many people struggle because they never really learn how to grow God's Spirit within them. It is like trying to gain muscle mass. You must work it out to build it in. You must connect with it and spend time cultivating it, to see the strength in it, manifest. The Spirit of God within you feeds off its connection to God and godly things. Spending time reading the Word of God is a sure way to build the Spirit within you. Spending time reading and discussing the Word of God with your spouse/significant other is another way to build the Spirit within you and your spouse/significant other. When you build the Spirit of God within you, it becomes the built-in filter that assesses the thoughts you have and identifies what is good for you and what needs to be discarded. It catches all the bad or foreign things and only lets the good things in that were meant to be deposited into your spirit and heart. The Spirit of God helps you to guard your heart against toxic or negative thoughts because it will not receive what is not kin to it. As you begin to utilize the Spirit of God in your thought process, you will begin to identify the thoughts that the enemy has tried to sneak into your marriage or relationship to destroy it. Remember, godly thoughts should always be deposited into your heart and spirit. They will feed and prosper you, but they will also do the same for your marriage/relationship.

Chapter Two
Thoughts from the Enemy

Just as God wants us to experience an abundant life, the Word says, *"The enemy comes to steal, kill and destroy".* For any believer, there is nothing truer than this Scripture. Many of us have suffered loss at the hands of the enemy. He is as unnoticeable as carbon monoxide, and just as deadly to our spirit and thoughts when not guarded. Every negative thought can be tied to the enemy because all negative thoughts come to steal, kill or destroy, especially those relative to your marriage/relationship. Whether the negative thoughts you have had have stolen the joy, love, commitment, or happiness in your marriage/relationship, you have the power and authority to gain it back. Perhaps, you have allowed them to even kill or destroy the passion and desire for your spouse that you once had. I'm here to tell you that you can absolutely get it back and take control of your marriage/relationship. Don't give in to the tricks of the enemy. He can be very cunning. You have the power in God to restore it all simply by changing the way you think about the whole situation and controlling your thoughts about your marriage/relationship.

Earlier, we discussed that all godly thoughts should be deposited into your marriage/relationship, well, the opposite should be applied for enemy driven thoughts. **Any thoughts generated by the enemy should never, ever be accepted and deposited into your marriage/relationship!** The surest way to determine if your thoughts are from the enemy is to compare them to what the Word of God says. Anything that contradicts the Word of God isn't God's thoughts but the enemy's. We know that to be true when the devil tempted Jesus in the wilderness in Matthew 4:1-11. Everything that he presented Jesus with, Jesus gave him a thought from God that held the truth. Let's look deeper; God's Word teaches us not to be selfish but to be selfless in our relationships with others. The enemy comes in and tries to create selfish thoughts within us especially when we are feeling neglected or ill-treated by our spouse/significant other. He will begin to have us thinking, our spouse/significant other is so selfish. That we should focus more on ourselves and our needs because our spouse/significant other is not going to meet them for us anyway. He will tell us that our spouse/significant other is not enough for us and we can do better than them by cheating or leaving our marriage/relationship. Thoughts from the enemy will always try to persuade you that there is better for you outside of your marriage/relationship than what you have. These thoughts will always highlight a fault or deficit in your spouse that is presented as something they are incapable of changing. Thoughts from the enemy fuel un-forgiveness, resentment, anger, revenge, and hate while godly thoughts fuel peace, forgiveness, grace, understanding, and love. **Any thoughts that you may currently hold in your heart about your marriage/relationship that is stealing, killing, or destroying it, is a thought from the enemy.** It is poison to a marriage/relationships ability to remain healthy and strong. If thoughts about your marriage are destroying the way you feel about your spouse, you have begun to deposit those negative thoughts into your heart which has manifested in your reality, exhibited by the way you feel and speak about your spouse.

Recently, there was a couple we were coaching that saw their marriage from a very negative lens. Everything that they said about it was negative, even when we prompted them to share something positive about it. As hard as they tried to think of something positive to say, they could not because they had flooded their hearts with negative thoughts so much, that it covered any positive thoughts that existed. They had allowed every godly thought to be blocked by the thoughts the enemy had been feeding them, and their filter was now controlled by the enemy. Now, while this couple was facing some trying times in their marriage for the last few years that could easily begin to birth negative thoughts for each of them, they made no effort to acknowledge or identify any good that had taken place or was taking place in their marriage. At this point in the marriage, they were guarding their hearts against all godly thoughts and only allowing thoughts from the enemy to be planted into their hearts and manifested into their lives. When we began to show them the pattern and effects of their thoughts, they were astonished that they had been feeding such negative thoughts into their marriage daily. They didn't realize the impact that their thoughts were having on their marriage and the ability those thoughts had to make it stronger or weaker. The Word of God says, *"Be alert and of sober mind. Your enemy the devil prowls around like a roaring lion looking for someone to devour." (1 Peter 5:8)*. What this teaches us is that the enemy is always roaming the earth looking to deposit his negative thoughts into someone's mind, and someone's marriage/relationship. His goal is to destroy it by changing the way you see it. We must be alert, at all times, about the thoughts that we have. The enemy will try to get you relaxed. He will tell you that the thought is a harmless one and everyone feels the way you do. **No negative thought is ever harmless.** Thoughts from the enemy always have the potential for damage when you accept them in your heart. Being of sober mind here is speaking to controlling your emotions. Many people struggle with controlling their thoughts because they have no control over their emotions. Think about it; if you are easily angered, the thoughts that you have during these times will not be godly ones. The enemy will feed you thoughts to continue to have you rest in emotions that he can use against you. The Word of God says to be, *"Quick to listen, slow to speak and slow to become angry because human anger does not produce the righteousness that God desires" (James 1:19-20)*. If anger doesn't produce what God desires, who desires it? Who would use it against us to destroy us? Yes, the enemy. Controlling your emotions is a sure way to control the enemy's ability to speak to your mind and heart. I'm not saying that we all may not have moments of pain, hurt, discouragement, doubt or anger, but do not linger there for the enemy to become roommates with you. *Ephesians 4:26 says, "And "don't sin by letting anger control you." Don't let the sun go down while you are still angry.* God knows that a lack of control over our emotions can easily result in us being controlled by thoughts from the enemy which can cause us to sin. Most marriages/relationships that you may see struggling with forgiveness, patience, or love have begun to accept what the enemy has fed them and no longer take control over their emotions. Emotions are natural and good when they rest in God. Never accept that you have no power in controlling your emotions. When you control your emotions, it keeps you on guard to control your thoughts.

So, what do we do with thoughts from the enemy? The Bible says to, *submit yourselves therefore to God. Resist the devil, and he will flee from you (James 4:7)*. Sounds easy, right? Anytime you resist the thoughts of the enemy you are protecting your marriage/relationship from the tricks of the enemy. In the Bible, we see Jesus do this, in a conversation with the devil after He fasted for 40 days. The enemy tried to tempt Him with His thoughts. He tried to get Jesus to believe what he was telling Him so that He would react a certain way and follow him. Jesus understood that the enemy's words/thoughts did not align with the thoughts of God. He began to compare the thoughts of the enemy with the thoughts of God. **To truly resist the enemy's thoughts, you have to learn how to effectively counter his thoughts with God's thoughts**. This is what submission to God looks like. For instance, when the enemy tells you that you may as well get divorced because it won't work out, you can counter the thought with, *"Therefore what God has joined together, let no one separate (Mark 10:9)"*. When the enemy tells you, you don't have the energy or strength to repair your marriage, counter it with, *"I can do all things through Christ who strengthens me (Philippians 4:13)."* When the enemy wants to tempt you with thoughts of infidelity, remind yourself that, *"Marriage should be honored by all, and the marriage bed kept pure, for God will judge the adulterer and all the sexually immoral" (Hebrews 13)*. Your submission to God's word is what helps to resist the devil and causes him to flee. **The Word of God is the most effective tool that can be used to resist the enemy and any negative thought he tries to plant within your heart and within your marriage/relationship.** While it may be easy to counter the enemy when he contradicts the Word, what happens when the enemy uses a part of the Word to shift your thoughts? With Jesus in the wilderness, he quoted a scripture found in the Bible to try and tempt Jesus. While what the enemy was saying is true scripture, the context in which he was using it, was not. Be careful, the enemy will use the Word of God to persuade you that what he is saying is true, but you must know the Word of God more than him to not be tricked. You must spend time reading the word individually and collectively so that you are not easily tricked by the enemy. You must ask God for understanding and revelation of His Word so that you know how to adequately apply it to your life and use it against the enemy.

The Enemy Uses the Past Against You

No one becomes an adult without building a past behind them. We all have a past that haunts us at times or reminds us of what we have overcome or been through. Our past can be used to make us better or bitter for our marriage/relationship. While many of you know that God can take our pasts to make us grow stronger and become better, the enemy has a purpose for our past as well. His goal is to take the past and attack you with it in a way that keeps you stuck and defeated. He uses our past thoughts to damage our present relationships. The enemy will always use past struggles and hurts to validate the negative thoughts he wants you to deposit into your present marriage/relationship or circumstance. For example, if you have a thought about your spouse cheating, the enemy will remind you of past relationships that ended with infidelity and try to confirm this thought in your current relationship even if it is untrue. **That is why it is important to heal from and deal with your past so that it has no influence on your present, and no control of your future.** When we don't take the time to heal from the past, the enemy takes hold of insecure moments in our lives and uses them against us. He wants you to believe that because you may have experienced infidelity in the past, it must be a part of your present marriage. He will try to convince you that you can't help but attract people that will steal, kill and destroy your love and spirit. This is a lie. Your past is your past and should only be used to praise God for the growth and lessons learned from it. When you choose to lie down with your past and rest in it, you slowly kill the present status of your relationship or marriage. Anytime the enemy tries to chain you to your past, ask God to release you from it. God is the chain breaker and anything you bring to Him that should not be connected to you; presently, God will remove. Past thoughts should never drive current thoughts about your current marriage/relationship. Live in the moment of your marriage/relationship so that what you experience is true of what is occurring today.

The Enemy's Deception

Many people find it hard to really guard their thoughts against the enemy because they expect the attack to be visible. Many expect to see alarms blazing in their minds when the enemy attempts to deposit something into them that they miss the true ways the enemy attacks. When the enemy attacks, it doesn't always seem like a heightened danger. He begins to deceive you about your marriage/relationship with small subtle things. He may start by building mistrust between the two of you. It may be shutting down communication in your marriage/relationship, and so you begin to start a friendship conversing with someone else of the opposite sex. It can be something as simple as making you feel alone and vulnerable in the marriage or relationship. Think about it this way; the enemy moves like carbon monoxide. It is not something you can see or smell with your natural senses much like the enemy. Carbon monoxide sneaks up and can only be detected by what was created to notice and identify its presence, a carbon monoxide detector. When carbon monoxide begins to infiltrate a home that does not have a carbon monoxide detector, all those in the home are at risk of being harmed and dying from the fumes that are secretly depositing themselves into their lungs and body. Now, for a home that has a working carbon monoxide detector, as soon as it is noticed or identified in the air of the home, the detector alerts the family that something dangerous is present that they cannot see. It prevents a harmful situation from occurring. That is what God and His Spirit are to our thoughts, and preventing thoughts from the enemy. God has created something in us that can notice and identify the enemy's presence in our lives. When you are connected to God, He is the carbon monoxide detector to the thoughts of the enemy. He has released His Spirit within us all to identify a threat before it attacks us. So, when you can't see the magnitude of the threat, He is able to block it before it hurts you. Most marriages/relationships suffer when they do not ensure that the Spirit of God is charged and working in their lives and their marriage/relationship. The Spirit is only as good as the source you connect it to. You must keep it connected to God and His Word to ensure that it is charged and ready to go when you need it. When the Spirit is charged in your life, no negative thought can take residence in your heart. Even if one can make it into your mind, the Spirit of God will filter it out and discard it before it has time to deposit itself into your heart and damage your marriage/relationship.

God's Presence Blocks the Enemy's Power

The more you are in the presence of God, the less power the enemy can have in your life. You can only fight against or counter the enemy's thoughts by allowing yourself to be in the presence of God. In the Bible, we read about David, who was called a man after God's own heart. As we read about David, we learn that he became attracted to someone else's wife and as the king, he felt that he could sleep with her and send her back home. To quickly summarize the story, the woman became pregnant with David's baby, and he had her husband killed. In this moment, David sinned against God, and in Psalms 51, he asked God not to remove His presence from him. Why was the presence of God so important to David? Perhaps, he understood that even in his sin and shortcomings, there was no way to live out a godly life and an abundant life without the presence of God. God's presence releases His thoughts which have power over the thoughts of the enemy just as God has power over Satan. The presence of God can block any other negative thoughts that can come your way, even after you have sinned. You see, the presence of God holds you accountable for any prior sins you may have committed from your thoughts, but it also restores and blesses you again in the end, like God did with David. Don't let the enemy convince you that just because you may have sinned with a thought that you accepted from him, that you can never have a godly thought again or that God will remove His presence from you. Remember the enemy's thoughts are full of evil and only have the power to release destruction in your marriage or relationship. You have the power through God and the Holy Spirit to ensure that the enemy doesn't use his thoughts to steal, kill or destroy the blessings in your marriage/relationship.

Chapter Three
Thoughts from Others

The third area, where we receive our thoughts are from other people. Thoughts from others can be beneficial as well as detrimental to you and your marriage/relationship, depending on the type of thought it is. Thoughts from others will either be negative or positive. They will either speak life or death to your union. They can be given to you by a deposit from God or a deposit from the enemy, so it is important to assess what type of thought it is. When we receive thoughts from others, we must truly determine whether the thought is something positive that will build us up or something negative that will steal, kill and destroy us or our marriage/relationship. Thoughts from others must always be filtered before you decide to receive them and deposit them into your heart. While most people have the best intentions when giving advice or sharing their thoughts, some people will advise you from their brokenness, which only allows them to see things from a negative, defeated, or hopeless place. Think about it, if you are facing something in your marriage/relationship and you are trying to feel hopeful about it, why would you receive a thought or advice that speaks hopelessness or defeat? No one can give power to an external thought but you. You are the gatekeeper to the thoughts that you receive into your mind and heart that can impact your marriage/relationship.

In the world we live in, we are very social beings. Our need to socialize opens us up to the opinions and thoughts of others. We begin to share with them our personal views and challenges. Once that door is opened, others will typically begin to share with you the thoughts and views that reside within them. This is a process that must take place for us all, but it is not a process that we must participate in without due diligence to guard our hearts. We must not get so comfortable and lost in the conversation that we leave ourselves open to anything being deposited into our hearts right under our noses. No, we must pay attention to every word, suggestion, and viewpoint that is sent our way from others that we converse with. Currently, we have become masterful in guarding thoughts from others, but it has not always been an easy thing to do. To be successful in managing and maximizing thoughts from others, there are some things that you must learn how to do along the way. Assessing the source, guarding all entry points, trusting what you know about yourself, avoiding pretenders, and surrounding yourself with others that think like where you are or where you desire to be is key. This will help you master how to profit from the thoughts of others in your marriage/relationship, and how to avoid being destroyed by their toxic thoughts that may be out of alignment with your destiny and thoughts.

Assessing the Source

The enemy as we stated earlier is very cunning. When he begins to see that you may have a handle on your thoughts, he will use those around you that you may trust and know to be wise, to deposit his thoughts into your mind. *Ephesians 5:6 says, "Do not let anyone deceive you with foolish words".* Simply meaning, do not believe any and everything without assessing its worth and purpose in your life. If it doesn't align with what you know to be true of yourself and your destiny, do not accept it into your life. You must watch who you lend your marital or relational ear to. While many of us may have the best intentions, we can easily give the worst advice to someone else. Be wise concerning who can speak into your life, marriage, or relationship. Many marriages/relationships fail not because of what is going on in the marriage/relationship, but because of what those around them have convinced them is going on in the marriage/relationship. No one can perceive what is taking place in your marriage or relationship better than you. All you must do is begin to have the right thoughts about it and guard yourself against thoughts from others that are not true. Every thought received from someone else stems from a godly thought or a thought from the enemy. You must be diligent in assessing where it comes from. Never take a thought from someone else without first asking God to confirm or refute the thought that was given to you. God is always there to guide us and ensure that what we are taking in is part of His plan and purpose for our life which is inclusive of our marriage/relationship.

The Word of God says, *"He will bring to light what is hidden in darkness and will expose the motives of the heart (1 Corinthians 4:5).* What may seem like good advice or a good thought from someone may be hidden in darkness that we sometimes, can't see because we trust and respect the person delivering the message to us. This doesn't make the person a bad person for they may not even realize that their thought pattern is flawed. Therefore, you must do the work to filter every thought from another person given to you concerning your life, marriage, or relationship. There should be no one in your life that gives you a thought that God and His Word cannot overrule. I mean, absolutely no one. God should have the ultimate power and say concerning what you allow into your heart that can affect your marriage/relationship. While there is no way to ensure that every thought from someone will be godly, you can start by first ensuring that the person you are lending your ear to has a relationship with God. If God cannot speak into their lives and change them, why should you take their advice in the first place? If God is not present in their marriage/relationship, what kind of godly thought could they possibly give to you? You must assess the source. Ask questions about that person's life that will reveal to you who they are and how they think. When you begin to learn more about the thoughts they have regarding marriage/relationships and assess how they live that area of their life; you can begin to determine if this is indeed someone that can add value to your thought bank concerning your marriage/relationship. We have come to realize that everyone is not worthy of the right to speak into our life concerning our marriage. This is not arrogance or pride. It is, in fact, a true understanding and value for what God has entrusted us with and gifted us to receive on earth. You must adopt this same mindset; no matter how close they are to you. Whether you have known them for 5 years or 35 years, they must be assessed. Whether they are family or friends, they must be assessed. When you make it a habit to assess those who look to deposit into your thought bank, you begin to remove people from your life who do not add value to your thought banking system. The goal is to win in marriage and to win in your relationship. Winning is a mindset that is fed by the thoughts that we have. If those around you have no desire to win or feed you winning thoughts, they have no right to capture your listening ear.

In our journey of coaching couples in marriage and relationships, we have found that some find it hard to receive what we tell them in our sessions. For some, it seems so farfetched and impossible because they cannot first begin to wrap their thoughts around the possibility of it. Many find it hard to believe that God can restore their marriage or that giving your spouse more of what you want out of the marriage will bring them to a place of reciprocity. We have learned that the issue is not in what we are teaching them. The issue is not in what God can allow them to create in their lives, but the issue stems from their belief that they, in fact, deserve that in which they currently do not have, but desire. Thoughts from others only hold power from the level in which you believe them to be true. When you are accustomed to receiving deadly thoughts about your marriage/relationship, thoughts that bring life to it can seem abnormal and unrealistic because you have resolved to die, and now, someone has advised you that life is possible. When someone gives you a godly thought to apply to your marriage/relationship, once you believe it, it now has the power to become your thought and manifest in your life. If you cannot believe it and receive it, you do not have the right to possess and birth it. Your thoughts are the bridge from what you desire, to what you experience in your marriage/relationship. If you expect nothing from it, it will give you nothing in return. If the thoughts that govern your marriage/relationship are limitless, you will experience a limitless marriage/relationship. 1 Corinthians 2:14 further proves this point. It states that *"the person without the Spirit does not accept the things that come from the Spirit of God but considers them foolishness."* What possibilities and promises from God concerning your marriage or relationship are you considering foolish? Who has been speaking life around you when all you can conceive and process is death? God has always been in the business of blessing us through our associations and relationships. This is true of transforming our thoughts as well. While you must take the time to assess those who speak into your life, ensure that you receive what they say once you have assessed that their thoughts are aligned with what God has been speaking to you and with what you desire for yourself. Guard your heart against those who should not have access but open it to those who are carrying beautiful treasures that will alter your thoughts in a way that manifest greatness in your marriage/relationship.

Guarding All Entry Points

It is important to note that thoughts from others are not solely received from the interactions of people in conversations. In the technological world, we live in; it is easy to receive thoughts from others through many platforms. Thoughts from others have many entry points into our lives, and if we are not careful to understand what they are and how to filter them, we can leave ourselves open to receiving these toxic thoughts from others that can negatively impact our marriage/relationship. Some of the entry points where thoughts from others impact our lives are through television, radio, books and especially social media. Many people today watch TV in their homes which is fine. Many homes have TVs in every room so that someone can tune into their favorite show without disturbing others. Many people watch hours of television a week, and many people watch it for what they call entertainment. Entertainment television has also now transformed into reality television that poisons the minds of many individuals today. Now, by no means are we advising you not to watch television as we are partakers in occasional TV watching, but you must not blindly and unconsciously indulge in watching TV, that you take no account of what is being deposited into your mind and heart. There is so much garbage on TV that goes against what a healthy marriage/relationship is. So many reality TV shows are teaching others that monogamy is only an illusion and not a possibility that more and more people are settling for infidelity in their relationship/marriage because they are being consumed with thoughts that having anything other than that is impossible. What you spend your time watching has the potential to alter your thoughts and can impact your marriage/relationship. **Feeling your mental space with chaos, confusion, conflict, infidelity, anger, separation, and selfishness delivered by a TV show, can impact your marriage/relationship negatively, if you are not careful to guard your thoughts.** You may find yourself agreeing with negative scenarios presented in a TV show at times because you have now unconsciously accepted the narrative they have painted for you and the rest of the world. After seeing so many episodes dealing with trust issues, you begin to have trust issues in your marriage/relationship. Guard your thoughts. You must see the TV as someone who can deposit thoughts within you so that you begin to filter what you watch and how it impacts your life.

While television has its impacts on our thoughts, so does radio and music. Many of us listen to the radio, and many of us now control what we listen to through music apps on our phones or in our vehicles. If we feel like listening to uplifting music, we connect to it. If we are feeling sad and depressed, we may tune into music that explains or justifies how we feel. If we are feeling romantic and in love, we may connect to that for the day, and if we are spiritually filled or seeking fulfillment, we may connect with some form of gospel music to support our feelings. These genres through radio can impact the thoughts you have about your marriage/relationship. **While it is great that we have more control over what we want to hear, we must be diligent in ensuring that what we want to hear aligns with what we need to hear to keep our thoughts in line with our destiny.** I've heard people say that music is the window to the soul, so what happens if the soul attached to the music you are listening to doesn't represent the thought patterns you need to become or remain successful in your marriage or your relationship? What if that soul is a defeated soul in the arena of marriage/relationships and their music echoes the unbelief within them of experiencing something beautiful? Everything created by someone else stems from thoughts that have driven that creativity. When you listen to music created by someone else, you are listening to their thoughts - what they believe. Whether what they believe is true or not, you have now given them access to your listening ear. You must be diligent in ensuring that what you listen to aligns with what you desire to have in your marriage/relationship. If you listen to something that is contrary to what you believe or desire, you must ensure that you do not deposit those thought patterns from the music you are listening to into your everyday thought patterns. Many people believe that we become what we see, but we also believe that you can become what you listen to. Ensure that the thoughts being delivered to you from others via the music you listen to impacts your marriage/relationship for good.

The most destructive and constructive entry point for many of us today regarding thoughts from others lies in social media. Social media is part of the life of almost everyone we are connected to. To understand the impact social media has on our lives and thoughts today, we can look at the overutilization of social media by our current president. Social media is one of those things that have great benefits and greater negative impacts. It has the potential to be used to build others and the same capacity to tear others down. It can be used to share vital information and can also be used to share toxic untrue information. **Of all the areas to guard concerning thoughts from others, this is the most overlooked, yet the most influential to marriage/relationships.** When you partake in social media, you open yourself up to the thoughts and opinions of others. With every post, you open yourself up to the unsolicited thoughts of others. If we are not careful, we can begin to blur the lines between what we think and what others think. Some people spend so much time on social media feeding themselves the thoughts of others that they no longer can determine where their true thoughts on an issue begin and where the thoughts of others that they have read all day end. Today, everyone is a marriage/relationship expert on social media. Those who have never had a successful marriage, let alone a successful relationship are now creating platforms where they are sharing their so-called expertise with others who are fascinated by their speech to the point they are blinded to their reality. Your thoughts can easily be influenced by others on social media especially when you admire or find value in their thoughts or behaviors. Thoughts delivered to you by others on social media must go through the same rigorous filtering system that thoughts from friends and families go through. Never blindly accept a thought from someone on social media that you have not vetted through God's thought filtering system that resides within you. Do not ignore the feelings you have that say this just doesn't make sense. Do not ignore the pull within you that tells you this person's thoughts do not align with your destiny, desire, or divine understanding. Take the time to research those whom you allow yourself to be fed from. Just because they have a platform does not mean their platform has a purpose in your life. Use social media wisely and take the time out to disconnect from it so that you can remain true to your thoughts and not be consumed with the thoughts of others. Social media is simply an entry point that delivers thoughts from others to your mind and heart. Guard the level of time and access you give this entry point so that your marriage/relationship is not negatively impacted by the overwhelming thoughts of others.

Trusting What You Know and Avoiding Pretenders

I have always been confused by people who let other people define them. How can someone on the outside of your physical and spiritual being inform you of who you truly are? I have always believed that to know who you are, you must dig deeper within yourself for God to reveal to you exactly who you are. To prevent thoughts from others from negatively impacting your life, marriage or relationship you must trust what you know about yourself. You must trust what you know about your marriage/relationship. You must know who you are and what you stand for. When you trust what you know about yourself, it is hard for someone to come and create another version of you and sell it to you as truth. Thoughts from others are only helpful when they confirm what you already know, not when they destroy what you know within your heart to be true. When you know who you are, it is easy to spot and avoid pretenders. Pretenders are people who give you thoughts that they do not live by, evident by their inability to obtain what they wish to teach you. Anyone that has truly mastered a thought around an issue will have that thought lived out in their life. It will be visible for others to see how the belief in the thought has now manifested itself in their lives. That is why companies looking to become successful usually go out and hire someone outside of their company to train their staff members on how to become successful. Not because they can say it well, but because they have proven, through manifestation, the thoughts they had about being successful. Anyone that is trying to deposit a thought about something that you desire or that is part of your destiny in your life should have a visible manifestation of that very thing in theirs. People who want to be successful want successful people telling them how to do it. **This is because people can only feed you from what they have stored inside of them.** Meaning, if I'm filled with the Spirit of God, my thoughts and advice will more than likely be driven by it. But if I am filled with evil and hate, my thoughts and advice, will be driven by those components as well. Anyone that you lend your ear to for advice or guidance needs to reflect that in which you desire to have already in their lives. Taking advice from someone else who is struggling in an area where you are struggling is like agreeing to drown together. This person cannot help you. They are unable to control their own thoughts in a way that allows them to be successful in their own marriage/relationship, so there is no way that they can now advise you on how to do so. Stop taking advice from impostors. If you desire a successful marriage/relationship, believe that you deserve it. Begin to expect it, and then, only allow thoughts from those who live it to be implemented into your life.

Others Who Think Like Where You Are or Desire to Be

It is true that winners surround themselves with winners and losers surround themselves with losers. Simply put, birds of a feather flock together. If you are desiring to gain thoughts that will elevate the current state or your marriage/relationship from others, you must begin to surround yourself with others that have the same mindset as you or those whom you aspire to be like. This goes back to the teaching of having a marriage circle/relationship circle around you from our first book, *Married by God: God's Blueprint to a Successful Marriage*. **Your circle of influence has the potential to propel you forward into what you currently think or what you want to think.** Whatever you desire about your marriage/relationship should line up with the type of people you have around you. It is insane to say that you want to experience a committed, loving marriage, but the friends in your circle all enjoy and embrace being unfaithful in their marriages. It is impossible to experience abundance in marriage when your circle of influence all sees obstacles and barriers regarding financial freedom in marriage. There is no reason to waste intimate time with people who are draining the thoughts that you need to have to live out what you believe in your heart. You owe it to yourself and your destiny to surround yourself with people and thoughts that will feed you daily so that you will begin to grow and bear fruit that can feed others as well. Our marriage circle is very tight. When I say tight, I mean extremely tight. There are very few people with the mindset that we have regarding our expectations in marriage, so we keep our circle powerful, but small. Les Brown has been known to say, "there is a difference from those who want something and those who expect something. Want shows up in conversation, expectation shows up in behavior." Our marriage circle is only full of people who expect to live out a blessed, prosperous, limitless life and that life is inclusive of a blessed, prosperous limitless marriage. Your thoughts cannot be thoughts of want; they must be thoughts of expectation. When you expect things to happen in your life and surround yourself with people who expect those things to happen for you as well, those things are released to you. You manifest them in your life because you create the environment that can create it and sustain it. Do not take for granted the mindsets of those around you. If it does not align with what you believe in your heart, validated by God then keep moving and find a circle big enough to expect to live out marriage/relationships on the level you know possible within your heart.

Chapter Four
Our Thoughts

There is nothing more challenging than assessing the thoughts that we give ourselves about our marriage/relationship. We typically can be the most critical and unrealistic when it comes to self-assessment. Everyone feeds themselves thoughts about their marriage or relationship. We tell ourselves that it is good, needs work, and even when we think it is beyond repair. But how accurate and true are our thoughts? I mean, we are the ones in the marriage/relationship, so we should know the truth about it right? Wrong. When you place your marriage in the hands of God, His thoughts become the only verifiable true thoughts that exist in your marriage. His Word says that His thoughts are nothing like our thoughts; in fact, it goes on to say that God's thoughts are higher than our thoughts. **If the thoughts of God are higher than our thoughts, could we possibly see things about our marriage/relationship on such a low scale that what we believe to be true about it isn't true at all?** Every thought you have about your marriage/relationship needs to be validated by God before you accept and deposit it into your heart.

His word says, in *2 Corinthians 10:5, "We destroy arguments and every lofty opinion raised against the knowledge of God and take every thought captive to obey Christ."* When you don't capture thoughts raised against the knowledge of God, you and your marriage/relationship become captive to them. What you don't capture, captures you! The thoughts you had about this possibly being a second failed marriage, have captured you. You are living it out by your thoughts. The thoughts you have about it being impossible to be happy and committed to one person, have captured you. All the negative thoughts you have deposited into your marriage or relationship are becoming fruits in it. You have the authority to take captive and align every thought about yourself, your spouse, your marriage, and your children with God's thought, and when you do that, you will begin to see all those things operate on another level. I am careful in my marriage about the thoughts I have regarding it especially in times of turmoil or discord. It is easy in these times to begin to tell yourself negative things regarding it, and to begin to believe them. Before you realize what has taken place, your behaviors towards your spouse begin to show what your thoughts about your marriage/relationship have become. Our actions are only reflections of what we deem to be true within ourselves. When we begin to believe the thoughts that our spouse/significant other does not value us or aren't enough for us, we can easily find ourselves in the arms of someone else. The act is only an effect. The cause is our ill thoughts that we have now accepted about our marriage or relationship. What you tell yourself about your marriage/relationship can positively impact it or negatively impact it. **It is important to note that your thoughts are not always decisive but that they can be deceptive.** *1 Corinthians 3:18 says, "Do not deceive yourselves. If any of you think you are wise by the standards of this age, you should become* *fools so that you may become wise. For the wisdom of this world is foolishness in God's sight."* Perhaps, what you believe to be true about your spouse, yourself, and about your marriage or relationship is wrapped in your own deception. Have you deceived yourself? Is your spouse as selfish as you say they are? Are they dishonest, angry, or as unreasonable as you profess? Do they really have a communication problem? Have they taken you for granted or have you undervalued yourself? Sometimes, what we refuse to acknowledge within ourselves, we begin to project on to those we love. We become fools to our own wisdom. **Never become so wise that your own wisdom deceives you.** You must take the time to dig for truth within yourself. That truth must be vetted through God to ensure that it is not driven by emotions that hold no true value or weight with the thought.

You have the absolute power regarding the thoughts you feed yourself. Those thoughts usually stem from what you have allowed to penetrate your mind from other entry points, and what you have allowed to be true about you from your past. Your past is only a piece of your life. While your experiences regarding your past are true, the past itself is not a true representation of who you are or who you desire to become. Anytime you let your past dictate what you can believe about your future, you begin to silence the thoughts that have the power to create your future. **Past circumstances can never have an impact on your present thoughts unless you authorize them to do so.** You determine the power that your past has on your thoughts. You can either agree with your past in a way that makes your present thoughts invalid, or you can disagree with your past so that your present thoughts are valid. You can truly decide to expect to have a successful second marriage, and that will be the only marriage you experience again until death. You have the power to do that. You also have the power to let your first failed marriage kill the success of your second marriage by the thoughts that you have about it. What is it that you are not expecting because of what you have experienced in the past? Perhaps, infidelity has stolen the expectation of fidelity in your current marriage; you must know that you have the power to change your reality by changing your thoughts. People who have successful marriages and relationships have successful thought patterns wrapped in expectation. I expect to have a blessed marriage with my husband. I expect him to be faithful to me and love me like Christ loved the church. I expect him to protect me and treat me well. I do not expect to be treated ill, and I do not expect to be betrayed by him. These thoughts have manifested into our marriage because my belief has fallen in line with what God has said I could have. You must expect it first to receive it.

Your expectation regarding your thought is what creates the behaviors that support and manifest what you desire in your marriage/relationship. Many times, we can feed ourselves fear that begins to suffocate expectation. Truly, fear teaches us not to expect, and in that lack of expectation, there is this false sense of safety from being hurt. In *2 Timothy 1:7, it states that "For God gave us a Spirit not of fear but of power and love and self-control."* Here, God shows that He wants you to expect things. He wants you to expect the thoughts that are aligned with Him to be birthed in your life, and you can birth those things with power, love, and self-control. Your thoughts have God's power behind them that when you believe them, you have the power to make the expectation become manifestation in your life. But you must first kill the threat of fear. You must place anything that you are afraid of daily on this scripture until you begin to believe what you are saying about it. Recite 2 Timothy 1:7 until what you say resonates in your thoughts so deeply, that it begins to become an expectation that you have. You have the power to determine what kind of marriage/relationship you will have. God has already released the power within you to make it happen, but you must come into alignment with Gods thoughts about you and your marriage/relationship to see it manifest in your life.

Build Yourself to Build Your Thoughts

I have been in the field of social work for over 13 years, and I am still surprised at the thoughts we feed ourselves about ourselves. Many people do not realize that the reason they feel defeated, hopeless, or invaluable stems from the words that they feed themselves daily. The marriages that are unhappy, falling apart, or in trouble are all fed from the individuals within them who find themselves unhappy, falling apart or in trouble. The seed is always a part of the fruit. Where there is bad fruit, there is also bad seed. If you want your marriage/relationship to be built stronger, you must build yourself up stronger first. That which you desire to see in your marriage/relationship, you must be able to believe and manifest it in your individual life. Your happiness does not begin with your marriage/relationship; it begins before it. The thoughts that feed your marriage happiness stem from the thoughts that feed you happiness. When you take the time to build yourself, it has a natural ability to build your marriage/relationship. If you desire to have peace in your marriage/relationship, start by creating peace within yourself. Your ability to transmit peace in your life will have a natural effect on transmitting peace within your marriage/relationship, as it is connected so closely to you. Most people desire to change their marriage or relationship from without but change always begins within. You must learn how to empower yourself in the very things that you desire to have within your marriage/relationship. I can recall a time I desired more romance in my marriage. I would constantly complain and fuss about the lack of romance in my marriage to myself as well as to my husband. I expected that the constant nagging and negative thoughts that consumed my marriage would have a positive effect on the romance in my marriage. This was misguided and ignorant thinking. After spending some time with God, I obtained a revelation that if I wanted more of what I desired, I would have to give more of that. I would have to create an atmosphere of romance consistently for my husband and I, so that it would naturally begin to change the atmosphere of my marriage. Now, I love God and His infinite wisdom, but the fleshly me was a little doubtful. Although I had some reservations about it, I have learned to listen to God more than my doubt, so I obeyed. I feed myself abundant thoughts of romance. I visualized my marriage full of romance daily. I began to do romantic things for my husband that I desired for myself. Over time, the atmosphere changed from one of discord over romance to one full of connection, love, and romance. My husband began to do the things I had done for him in return and even took it a step further and began to do things from his own creative mind. It all begins with changing your thought patterns within that drives your actions on the outside.

We live in a world today full of so many thoughts and ideas that have access into our everyday lives. Most times, if you don't constantly tell yourself who you are and what your marriage/relationship is the world will create it for you. You can find yourself reading magazines on the conditions of today's marriages/relationships. All of it may be negative, and you may not be aware that you are taking this into your own mind and thoughts. You may see TV shows or movies where marriages and relationships are struggling and find yourself believing that all marriages and relationships are a struggle. Before you know it, because you have begun to feed yourself these thoughts and beliefs, you begin to experience troubles and challenging times in your marriage/relationship. For instance, the culture today tells us that to have a solid marriage/relationship; you must go through some trying times. It is teaching our young girls that to secure a man; you must deal with his lying and cheating ways until he matures because all men do this. If you begin to feed yourself this picture and this mindset, then surely you will find yourself in a relationship or marriage experiencing the very things that you believe to be true. In contrast, if you believe that a healthy marriage/relationship only experiences joy, peace, love, patience, trust, commitment, and unity these are all the things that will begin to manifest in your marriage/relationship. As believers, we have become so comfortable in embracing life's circumstances that we forget the power that God gives us to create our own, which begins with our thoughts. As a man thinks in his heart so is he, is scripturally based and proven to be true in the many lives of those who understand how to make their thoughts work for them and not against them. It all begins with you. Learn to affirm only positive thoughts about your marriage/relationship to yourself. Begin to generate a list of affirmations that feed your thoughts daily on the great state that your marriage/relationship is in. I have learned to affirm my marriage every morning and night. I hold no shame or hesitance in proclaiming that I have a loving, prosperous, unified, Godly, limitless, outstanding, giving, protected, and wonderful marriage. You are your only limitation in experiencing what you desire in your marriage/relationship. Write a list of what you desire of your marriage/relationship and write it in a way that declares you already have it. Read this every morning and every night for 30 days and begin to believe and envision this in your marriage/relationship. If you have a little trouble in beginning, here are a few to get you started.

I Have a Healthy Marriage/Relationship.
I Have a Prosperous Marriage/Relationship.
My Marriage/Relationship is Full of Love.
I Trust My Spouse Because He/She is Trustworthy.
My Marriage/Relationship is Full of Joy, Peace, and Harmony.
God Covers my Marriage/Relationship Daily.
My Marriage/Relationship is Blessed Beyond Measure.

Avoiding Worthless Thoughts

Psalm 94:11 says, "The LORD knows people's thoughts, He knows they are worthless." God knows that unless our thoughts are validated by His wisdom, they are worthless thoughts. They hold no true value on what is real in our life or marriage. *When you produce worthless thoughts in your marriage or relationship, they create weight and worry.* The weight comes from all the untrue thoughts that you have attached to your marriage/relationship. It comes from what you have accepted to be true that has not been purified, tested, taken through the fire by God. Then it also creates worry. Worry is defined in the dictionary as, "giving way to anxiety or unease; to allow one's mind to dwell on difficulty or troubles." Another definition that I like better says, "a state of anxiety and uncertainty over actual or potential problems." Simply put, your worthless thoughts have created worry over potential problems. Not real problems, not current problems but potential problems. Those thoughts about potential problems begin to manifest real problems into your life because you have now begun to accept them in your mind and deposit them as true into your heart.

Point: When you do not filter your thoughts through God, they begin to attack you and your marriage/relationship.

You must always filter your thoughts through the spirit within you. The Spirit of God is the tool used to validate or refute the thoughts that we have. It helps to assess whether these thoughts are worthy or worthless. When you ignore the Spirit of God or spirit within you, you allow worthless thoughts to take residence within your mind and heart. Those worthless thoughts begin to germinate in your marriage/relationship, and you begin to see the fruits of those worthless thoughts take residence in your life. We all have worthless thoughts throughout the day. No one is free from it, and no one can avoid it. What we can do is to be mindful and aware of the thoughts we have so that when we receive a worthless thought, we are able to quickly catch and dispose of that thought before it takes residence in our spirit. If you find yourself currently feeling anxious, worried or heavy, you have allowed worthless thoughts to take residence in your mind and spirit. Begin to counter these thoughts with power thoughts. Take the time to identify the worthless thoughts and replace them with worthy thoughts. Worthy thoughts give your marriage/relationship life and are full of love and expectancy for beautiful and wonderful things. Remember that you are worthy of great love. You are worthy of experiencing joy, peace, and happiness, but you must first consume yourself with thoughts of worthiness to experience them in your marriage/relationship.

Chapter Five
Control Your Thoughts

If You Can't Control the Thought, Control What You Do with It

The first step in controlling what to do with your thoughts is to assess what kind of thought you are having. Is it a godly thought or a thought from the enemy? Is it a negative thought or is it a positive thought? The easiest way to determine it is to evaluate its impact on your feelings or emotions at the time that you think it. Does the thought make you feel loving and happy with your spouse? Does it make you feel hopeful for the union despite what you may be facing? If this is true, more than likely, the thought you are having about your marriage/relationship is positive or a godly one. On the other hand, if you begin to feel angry, anxious, discouraged or overwhelmed towards your spouse, then surely the thought is a negative thought or thought from the enemy. Remember, thoughts are not facts. Your facts are what you determine them to be through your thoughts. You can experience something negative in your marriage and choose to turn the negative feelings about it into positive ones, especially with the inclusion and understanding of God's will and purpose for your life. God's Word tells us that, "all things work together for the good of them that love the Lord and are called according to His purpose". When we understand this, then it can easily be applied to the thoughts concerning our marriage/relationship.

I am excited to have learned how to truly make all things work together for my good in my life and especially in my marriage. All things working together for the good begin with a mindset. It begins with the thoughts that no matter what I may face or go through, this situation must work out for my good because I desire it to and God wants it to work for me as well. Many of us never experience all things working for our good because we can't see past the negative thoughts we have about what we have experienced. If you can't see past the negative thoughts and create a positive outlook of goodness from them, you can never truly experience all things working out for your good. When you become aware of the power, God enables us all with; you will begin to tap into this power and create the marriage/relationship that you desire. In 13 years of marriage, my husband and I have had many situations not work out for the good, not because God didn't desire it to, but because we could not see or believe that they would. Your belief in the good is the very thing that manifests the good in your life. It is what takes the bad and wraps it in good for your benefit. God does not need you to see how it will work for your good. You do not need the details. All God needs from you is the belief that everything will work out for the good and continue to live your life as if the good has already happened. This is one of the best ways to control your thoughts.

Many people do not realize that the relationship and marriage that they experience has everything to do with their thoughts. While your thoughts hold all the power on what you manifest in your life, you hold all the power over the thoughts that you have; therefore, you control the outcome of your life and your marriage/relationship. Our emotions are an indicator of the thoughts that we are having about our marriage or relationships. If you want to learn to control your thoughts better, you must pay close attention to the feelings and emotions that you are having in your marriage/relationship. We were coaching a couple that had experienced infidelity and was dealing with building back trust within their marriage. The wife constantly would tell herself that her husband was untrustworthy numerous times a day. She would feed herself thoughts of mistrust and dishonesty. She would imagine the things that her husband may be doing while he was gone, although he was at work. She refused to believe that he could be truthful, so she kept the negative thoughts flowing in her mind daily around him being untrustworthy and unfaithful. On the other hand, the husband complained daily that his wife did not trust him and would never trust him again. He believed that no matter what he did or would do, she would never believe him or trust him again. He felt that rebuilding trust was a hopeless situation in their marriage and would never happen. What these two did not realize was that they were living and experiencing the very life that their thoughts now created for them. Both fed mistrust and doubt into their union daily, which in turn manifested for them daily. Their thoughts were the constant fuel needed for them to continue to get what they expected to happen. We worked with them to begin to change the thoughts that they were having and focus those thoughts on positively building trust and having trust within their marriage. Soon, they began to see the fruits of their labor as they feed each other and themselves positive thoughts concerning trust in their union. **We believe that you do not get what you deserve, but you get what you BELIEVE you deserve.** Neither of them believed that they deserved peace and reconciliation regarding the infidelity. They did not believe that they deserved to be in a union full of trust between them. Everything that they spoke reflected their thoughts. Their emotions and feelings reflected their negative thoughts, and the atmosphere of their marriage became a reflection of those very thoughts as well. If you desire to change the atmosphere of your marriage/relationship, change the temperature of your thoughts. Once your thoughts are programmed towards positivity and possibility, you begin to feel those thoughts manifest in your marriage/relationship.

Now, by no means do we want to convey that controlling your thoughts will initially be an easy task. In all truth, it will be one of the most challenging but rewarding things that you can do for your life and your marriage/relationship. When you learn how to control your thoughts about your marriage/relationship, it also controls the things that you allow into it, and it controls how you respond to situations that you face. When you learn to control your thoughts, you become empowered to live the marriage/relationship that you have always desired to have. For any couple desiring to learn how to control their thoughts, first begin by making a list of what you like and don't like about your marriage/relationship. Once you have generated a list on a scale of one to ten, rate how much you feel this is true with 1 being the least and 10 being the most. For every thought with a 5 or better, those are the thoughts that are ruling your marriage/relationship, and if you are honest, are the fruits that you see in them as well. For all the negative thoughts that you have, replace them with a positive, godly thought and begin to affirm that to yourself daily. An example is listed below to assist you in changing every negative thought into positive thoughts that can improve your marriage/relationship. While some of you won't believe in the process, many of you will complete the steps and begin to see the impact that it begins to have on your marriage/relationship.

My Husband is Very Inconsiderate. - Wrong Thought
I Have a Considerate Husband. - Positive/Correct Thought
I Am No Longer Attracted to My Wife. - Wrong Thought
My Wife Is the Most Attractive Woman Alive. - Positive/Correct Thought

To control your thoughts, you must learn how to direct where the thoughts go. When you are intentional about where your thoughts go, you become more aware of what thoughts to keep and what thoughts to discard. To experience a positive and joyful marriage/relationship, you must choose to retain every positive, godly thought about it and discard every (not just some) negative enemy thought about it. When you begin to analyze the makeup of your thoughts, you begin to guard your heart and take control of the thoughts you have. For instance, you may be experiencing a rough period in your marriage/relationship. For the past few months, everything has seemed to have a negative impact on your marriage/relationship, and you are wondering how you got there. If you were to honestly reflect on the thoughts you had after every obstacle or trial you faced in the relationship/marriage recently, there you would find an abundance of negative thoughts driven by the enemy that have now taken residence in your heart. Your current feelings and actions towards your spouse are based upon your current heart thoughts. If you want to change how you see and feel about your marriage/relationship, you will have to change the way you think about it daily. Begin to discard every negative thought from the enemy by first, not affirming it and second, by choosing to dismiss it as untrue. **Whenever you attach truth to a negative thought from the enemy, you give it traction to take over and become real in your marriage/relationship.** Stop believing that a simple thought is harmless. Remember, every thought can add to or take away from the joy you experience in your marriage/relationship. So, discard every negative enemy-driven thought, swiftly. Deposit positive, godly thoughts in your heart so that you can meditate on those things and begin to see and experience your marriage/relationship in a positive light, guided by God. If your heart is overflowing with godly thoughts, you will view and experience your marriage/relationship positively. Remember, you are the navigator of your marriage/relationship.

The next step in controlling what to do with your thoughts is mastering the ability to spin a thought. **Spinning a thought is simply taking a negative thought and choosing not to discard it but to find the positive in it and use it for your good.** Spinning takes practice and commitment to execute properly. I can recall a time my husband and myself were arguing a lot. Both of us felt like we were not getting what we needed from each other at the time, and both of us were withholding what the other needed until we felt like we got our needs met first. Yes, immature and idiotic was the name of the game both of us were playing. During this time, I was so very frustrated with him and started to really dislike him. I mean REALLY! I went to God in prayer to change my husband, and God decided to change my outlook and thoughts about the situation instead. What He showed me was that this was an opportunity for me to practice what I preached about weekly on *Married by God*. That agape love that I knew like the back of my hand was the last thing in the world I wanted to give and think about now. God showed me that instead of looking at it as a rough time in my marriage, look at it as an opportunity to be Christ-like to my husband and truly walk in agape love. When I saw it from that perspective, I decided to handle the situation differently and saw the trial in my marriage as a gift to strengthen my relationship and commitment to God and my husband. **Remember spinning is winning.** The enemy would love for us to feel defeated when trials and tribulations come knocking at our marriage/relationship door. When we spin what the devil meant for evil and show him how God meant it for good, we strengthen our faith in God and strengthen our marriage/relationship with our spouse/significant other.

The ability to manage your thoughts begins with self-control. If you have no control over yourself, you will be easily led by your emotions, fears, and negative thoughts. Self-control allows us to determine and dictate what thoughts will influence our lives, especially our relationship or marriage. Self-control is a fruit of the Spirit that must be watered to become strong and effective in our walk with God. Every time you take the time to think about your thoughts, assess whether they are positive or negative, and determine what to do with it, you are building self-control in your life. Now, this won't be easy. There will be times in your marriage/relationship where you fail miserably to execute self-control. There will be times when your temper may flare, words you don't mean may be said, and actions you regret may be taken, but that is all part of the self-control journey. Anytime God wants to build an area in your life, He places you in situations that require the use of the very thing He is trying to build. So, if self-control is on your agenda, expect to have sometimes in your marriage/relationship that make you feel like you want to lose control or have lost control. In those moments, after the emotions have calmed a bit, spend some time with God to learn the lesson from the situation. Apologize for losing control to your spouse/significant other, and explain to them how you hope to handle the situation if it occurs again. When you can control yourself and control your thoughts, you begin to master the ability to destroy arguments and every lofty opinion raised against the knowledge of God. You then have the power to take every thought captive to obey Christ as the Bible says in 2 Corinthians 10:5. Imagine having the power to make your thoughts obey what God has spoken about your marriage/relationship. Imagine living abundantly, joyfully, peacefully, and in love in your marriage/relationship. Imagine living it out and experiencing the abundance and fullness of what God intended your marriage/relationship to be. Decide today to no longer be a victim of your negative thoughts but to take control of them.

As stated earlier, controlling your thoughts begins with an understanding of where the thoughts originate from. Our present thoughts may sometimes be influenced by past historical negative thoughts. Some of us have experienced tremendous amounts of hurt and pain at the hands of those who professed to love us that our thoughts about what a loving marriage/relationship should be, stem from those past hurtful and painful experiences. Have you ever known someone who so desperately professed to want a healthy relationship with someone but every relationship they entered was toxic and unhealthy? Their track record shows a list of unhealthy relationships with them being the only common denominator. How can someone desire one thing but experience what they claim they do not desire to experience? It is easy. It is all wrapped within their thoughts. As much as they profess to want to change, their thoughts have not changed; thus manifesting repeatedly, the things they claim they do not want in their marriage/relationship. Historical thoughts can be detrimental to a healthy marriage/relationship especially when they are full of negativity. Thoughts shape our mindsets about things, and they create the behaviors that we exhibit in our marriage/relationships. Someone who has experienced infidelity repeatedly in a marriage/relationship has dominant historical thoughts of infidelity present in their current marriage/relationship that will begin to shape and create that atmosphere in their present circumstance if they are not careful. They will begin to question their spouse or mistrust them. They will begin to look for signs of infidelity even if none are present. They will create this visual in their minds that it begins to manifest in their lives, and once the infidelity takes place again, they will justify the act by saying I knew men or women couldn't be faithful. Until their thoughts change, their experience will be the same. Gandhi said, "Your beliefs become thoughts." So, if you believe certain historical thoughts to be true because of your experience with them, they will become your present thoughts as well.

Avoid Regret

The surest way to control your thoughts is to avoid thoughts of regret. Thoughts of regret always have you living in past negative thoughts instead of a positive future or present thoughts. Prentice Mulford in Thoughts Are Things stated that "God does not regret and if we are made in His image and likeness we should not regret either." We could not agree more. God does not live in the past or past moments of our lives. God lives in our present thought and present circumstance. If you desire to control your thoughts in a way that helps you to focus on positive and godly thoughts, pay attention to the thoughts that try to drag you back to the past. Regrets always stem from a place of lack and a place of negativity. If you find yourself desiring a time in your marriage/relationship where things were better than they are now, you are taking away from any joyous moments you could be experiencing right now. **Regret robs you of a chance at present joy.** If you find yourself reflecting on a past relationship other than the current one you are in, you will begin to tell yourself thoughts that devalue the current relationship you are in. You will desire to be in a past relationship mentally that takes you away from your current one. We must be careful to understand that anything you regret, you have the potential to relive. If past relationships have been toxic or bad, don't regret being in them, just forget about them all together and enjoy the love within the current one you are in. If you are not in a current relationship, focus on the joy and love that is awaiting you in your next relationship. Regretting anything ensures that the thoughts that you are having are negative and defeating thoughts.

For instance, think of a time when you and your spouse/significant other argued. Let's say the argument was a bad one, but you both agreed to move past it. The next day, you find yourself regretting the argument and some things that you or your spouse said. Your thoughts at the time take you back to the space and atmosphere of the argument the day before. Instead of moving forward, you begin to feel angry or frustrated, and you cannot understand why. You want to continue the argument because your thoughts have dragged you back to yesterday. The only way to effectively control your thoughts is to make sure that you keep them in the present or future. Keep your mind on what you want to experience or what you are currently experiencing that is good. This will help you to see your marriage/relationship in a positive light and help generate those feelings of joy and hope that you need to sustain a long-term relationship/marriage.

Controlling our thoughts is key to experiencing the marriage/relationship that we desire. It is a vital ingredient to having what so many desires but can't seem to obtain in marriage/relationships, which is true Joy and Love. Bob Proctor said that "Thoughts become things. If you see it in your mind you will hold it in your hand." The Word of God says in Proverbs 23:7, "As a man thinks in his heart so is he." These two quotes show the power of our thoughts and the power in controlling our thoughts. You have the power to live the marriage/relationship you desire. You have the power to create the beautiful picture that resides within your mind or the dark gloomy defeating picture that lives there as well. **The canvas of your marriage/relationship is clean and ready to be painted by the thoughts that drive the brush strokes.** Be diligent in paying attention to your thoughts and discarding those that do not serve to create what you believe you deserve in your marriage/relationship. Imagine your marriage/relationship changing and improving one thought at a time and begin to manifest those thoughts into your reality.

Chapter Six
Believing in Blessed

Some of you have read the title of this chapter, and immediately, a negative thought ran across your mind and stole the possibility of this being true in your life. It's okay; it has happened to us all. We have all fallen victim to our historical thoughts. Your historical thoughts (which we discussed) are fighting against your current desires or beliefs, especially when you move from being driven by the enemy's thoughts to only embracing Godly thoughts. Before any of us can ever experience what we desire in our lives, we must believe that we deserve to have it like anyone else. **What you don't believe you don't get to experience.** God's Word is very clear. When you ask God for something in prayer, believing and having the faith that you will receive it, then it is done for you (Mark 11:24). That is scripture, and that scripture is a true and definitive fact. Many people ask to be blessed but do not believe that they are or that they will be. They begin to feed themselves counterproductive thoughts that go against the very thing that they just prayed to God for. God wants to give us the desires of our hearts, but we must believe that we deserve them and that we will receive them. This chapter will focus on experiencing a blessed and wonderful marriage/relationship in your thoughts, that will reflect it in your reality, when you know and believe that you are blessed.

Believing You Deserve It

Most people never experience all God has for them because they never truly believe in their heart that they are deserving of it. Most of us have given into the lies that true happiness and love does not exist in marriage/relationships anymore, and those that have it are part of the lucky few. A secret club that is no longer accepting members, so they become our idolized #Relationship Goals. Some of us have accepted the fact that a miserable marriage/relationship is all we will have, and it's better than being alone. This is nothing but a thought implanted by the enemy himself. **God doesn't desire for believers to live a defeated and mediocre life.** The Word of God says that He comes so that we may have life and have it abundantly. This abundant life isn't for selected believers. It is for all of them that diligently seek Him and believe that they can have it. Many people are failing in marriage or relationships not because they truly can't have a successful marriage/relationship. **They are failing because their belief system doesn't support the weight that having a successful marriage/relationship requires.** You cannot have a weak belief system as a foundation to support a strong and thriving marriage/relationship - it will not work. Those whom you may admire in marriage/relationships have only tapped into the power that their thoughts must align with their beliefs, which can manifest what they have asked God for. You have the same opportunity to construct a beautiful marriage/relationship just as the other person does. Your only limitation is the one that you set within your mind.

Believing that you deserve good and can experience a good marriage/relationship can be challenging especially when the majority of the union has been defined by tough times. As a believer, your belief system cannot be based off what you see. It must be rooted in what God promises. His promises are what we must build our belief's on, for His promises do not change. God is the same yesterday, today, and forever more and so is His word. If what God promises don't change, then the only thing that could have changed was your belief in God's promises. Anything that is delayed in our lives we immediately want to tie it to the enemy or to it not being Gods timing, but perhaps, it is tied to our thinking. Perhaps, what you desire to have isn't being released because you truly don't believe you can have it nor deserve it. Those who feel they deserve something do not settle for anything less than what they feel they deserve. This belief in deserving is what brings those very things into their life. Someone who feels that they are blessed daily will feel blessed daily no matter what happens that day. Because they believe they are blessed, they will be able to pinpoint something in their day that confirms their level of belief. The same is true for someone who feels like life is beating them up or everything is going wrong. Because they so deeply believe that things always go wrong for them, they will be able to pinpoint something wrong daily.

Seeing it Before You Experience It

We must understand that our thoughts have manifestation power. It is important to speak things that you want to experience before you ever experience them. Paul says, "To speak those things that are not as though they were." This is the power of believing in your thoughts and manifesting it in your life. Perhaps, your marriage/relationship is not full of joy, peace, and love at this moment, but use your transforming power to speak it as if it is. Train your thoughts to believe that your marriage/relationship is full of love, joy, and peace and you will begin to experience those things within it. This is not magic; it is not imaginary. These are biblical principles and universal laws that many believers just do not utilize. Everything you desire, you have the power to create. So many of us have been weighed down by religious teachings that we never truly tap into the spiritual connection and power that is God. We look for things to happen outside of us instead of looking to tap into our God power and make things happen from within us. Instead of connecting with God in prayer by aligning our thoughts with His, we just pray and put all the responsibility on God. When nothing happens, we go back, pray again and wait. All the while, God is waiting for your thoughts to align with His so that His power can be transmitted to you for you to begin to act and change things. Our relationship with the almighty God is not an outward one but an inward one. We must be diligent in making sure that our thoughts are aligned with what we know God wants for us and has already released for us to have.

We walk by faith and not by sight is a principle that can positively impact every area of our life. The ability to believe something so earnestly before it is ever proven in our lives is the foundation of our relationship and belief in God. It is the principle of faith that drives every believer to live the life they are called to live. Faith is a necessity and a benefit to every area of our lives, especially our marriage/relationship. Before you can ever experience a blessed marriage/relationship, you must have faith in your marriage/relationship. Believing that you possess a blessed marriage/relationship in your thoughts before it ever materializes in the flesh, is the beginning of manifesting the reality of it. I can recall for myself always knowing and believing that I would have a blessed and happy marriage. Through failed relationships and bad experiences, my faith in God and my belief in experiencing real love and commitment never left me. My ability to see my marriage as blessed before ever experiencing it has allowed me to reflect my thoughts into my reality through God. Every day, I can live a blessed, peaceful, loving, and joyful marriage because I believe it and my thoughts support my beliefs. You must learn to do the same if you want to have a beautiful union. No one can do it for you. You must create these thoughts and beliefs for yourself. We believe that no matter what the circumstances currently look like, Godly thoughts can transform and change it all. In the Bible, Jesus spoke to the disciples and said, *"If anyone says to this mountain, 'Go, throw yourself into the sea,' and does not doubt in their heart but believes that what they say will happen, it will be done for them"* *(Mark 11:23).* This reflects what we are speaking of here. You can do what many may deem as impossible. It begins with your belief that it can be done. The marriage/relationship that you desire is within you to believe and create. It takes great faith to manifest it, and without it, nothing will be created. If faith is what you are lacking, then you must take the time to build your faith in God. Building faith comes from spending time with God and having a real connection with Him. God is a God of evidence. When you are connected to Him, He begins to build your faith through evidence that you can see. Begin with trivial things that your current faith can handle. Ask God to change your thoughts in that area and begin to control the thoughts you are having to imagine the things that you want to see. Believe that God will allow it to happen and manifest. When your beliefs begin to align with your thoughts, you will begin to have the evidence you need to continue to grow in faith. **Understand that your belief in the bad has the same ability to manifest as your belief in the good.** Your thoughts will be the determining factor in what you see in your life, so why not believe for the best.

Understanding that you are blessed is the first step in believing that you are blessed. You are blessed whether you believe it or not. The blessing is there. Your inability to grasp that you are blessed does not negate that you are blessed, but it does prevent you from living and experiencing a blessed life, thus a blessed marriage/relationship. Knowing that you are blessed in God should be a motivation to begin to make your thoughts believe what God has already spoken. As a believer, I know that I am blessed and highly favored; therefore, I expect all areas of my life to reflect this belief and understanding. I ensure that my thoughts are supportive of this belief and my daily life has become a reflection of my thoughts and my beliefs. Even in the areas that have not visibly manifested now, my thoughts are supporting the belief that it will manifest for me because the God I serve has already given it to me. Every visual picture in my mind has become or will become my reality because it has no choice but to live up to God's Word. Believe it for yourself today and begin to unfold the life you desire.

The Power of Visuals

There was a time when imaginations would run wild among children and adults alike. As a child, I can recall reading books that would become so real from the visual pictures and scenes that I would paint in my head to support the stories that I read. We believe that imagination is a gift from God that allows you to see your future in your present state. It is a way to align your thoughts with what God desires for you in a very tangible way. Whatever you can imagine, you can create. As a designer, everything that I sew, I have visualized within my mind by my thoughts before it is ever sown from a piece of fabric. My thoughts create the masterpiece of clothing that many see today. Whether you are an artist, painter, songwriter, designer, or whatever, you have the gift of visualization within you waiting to be used. The marriage/relationship you desire is waiting to be created within your mind by your thoughts so that it can be birthed into the world. Can you see it? Can you see yourself along with your spouse/significant other living and enjoying life to the fullest? Can you see yourselves working together in a successful business? Can you see yourselves working together in ministry to help the world become better? If you cannot, you must truly take the time to work on your imagination and ability to visualize things. My husband and I started picturing ourselves in the cars we wanted doing things that we wanted to do together. We would both visualize a spot where we wanted to meet in our dream cars and move from scene to scene together. Laughing and loving each other along the way. These visions were very real to us, and some have manifested while others are very close to manifesting in our lives. Stop believing that you cannot create the marriage and relationship that you desire. You can, just imagine it!

Every year, people gather together to embark on the task of making a vision board. Their vision boards may include images and pictures that represent the things that they desire to have in their lives for the upcoming year. Those things may include homes, cars, vacations, children, businesses, spouses, feelings, wealth, spirituality and so much more. Vision boards are only our use of imagination put into a practical task. What we imagine in our thoughts, become the images we find and choose to represent on paper. For those who may be struggling to see all that their marriage or relationship could be, we recommend creating a vision board for it. First, you must visualize all that you desire for your marriage/relationship in your mind by guiding your thoughts to what you desire. Spend a day or two meditating for at least, 15 minutes on what you desire to see in your marriage/relationship. Once you have meditated on it, write the details out on a sheet of paper, and discuss them with each other. Next, spend some time finding the images or pictures that most likely represent the thoughts that you have had regarding your marriage/relationship. Caption it "Our Vision of Love". Everything on the board should be a positive representation of the positive thoughts that you have concerning your marriage/relationship. Place the vision board somewhere in your home where you both can see it and create thoughts that will help you achieve what you see on the board. Many people create vision boards and never really look at them or periodically check them to see if they are on track to creating what they desire. Have a vision check monthly with your spouse/significant other to discuss the progress that has been made, and to help ensure that your thoughts are supporting the marriage/relationship that you desire.

Chapter Seven
Alignment - My Priority is God's Priority

Often, I wish the things that I know to be true now I knew to be true 13 years ago when I first got married. As believers, many of us are taught that God loves us and wants the best for us. We learn that God cares about what happens to us and guides our lives as believers in Him. But many times, we are not taught that we are God's priority as believers. God is not just concerned about our souls, but He is concerned about every aspect of our lives including our marriage/relationship. We are not taught the importance of including God in our everyday affairs, especially as it relates to our marriage/relationship. If no one else has told you this, your marriage/relationship is a priority to God, especially when you include Him in it. A marriage built inclusively on God is placed on the agenda of God. When you are connected to God in such a way, your marriage/relationship is affected by Him in ways that you can't always immediately see. When your marriage/relationship is connected to the source that is God, every resource that you need is available for your use. Many of us don't realize that we are connected to the source that is God and that our thoughts begin to release all that He has in store for us to receive.

Some of us never really tap into the true power that a relationship with God provides. When you are connected to God in a way that talks to Him and seeks Him daily concerning your marriage/relationship, you help to align your thoughts with the thoughts of God concerning it. When you spend quality time with God, you allow Him to counter and negate every negative thought that may have slipped into your subconscious mind unnoticed. Those thoughts of insecurity, discord, hopelessness, failure, or rejection cannot stay in the presence of God for they do not align with the very nature of who God is. God is strength, confidence, success, prosperity, hope, and peace. **God will provide your marriage/relationship with what it needs when you seek Him.** Think about it, the same God that so effortlessly ensures that the birds of the air are provided for, takes the same time to ensure that you are provided for in a way that supports and improves your marriage/relationship (Matthew 6:26). The birds go on about their day knowing that they will be provided for. They don't sit and worry about what to do next and decide to get sad and stop flying. No, they continue to move on knowing and expecting things to work out for them. That is what God expects us to understand and know within ourselves and within our marriage/relationship. God is a provider in all things. He can ensure that you have what you need to have to keep your marriage/relationship thriving. If you are lacking the thoughts needed to sustain and grow your marriage/relationship, connect to the source which is God, for He has abundant knowledge and wisdom that can help guide you along the way.

God's Armor Equals Gods Thoughts

Many times, when we think of God, we never think of connecting with God in a way that connects us to His thinking and wisdom. *Ephesians 6:11 says, "Put on the whole armor of God, that you may be able to stand against the schemes of the devil".* What is the whole armor of God? We have been trained or taught to believe that the armor is just outward in nature. That we are to just read God's Word and recite it at times of trouble and those troubles will flee from us. What many of us find out is that it takes more than reading and reciting God's Word for it to have a transforming impact on our lives. The Armor of God we believe is being referenced here is inclusive of the mental armor of God. The thought process of God. To think as God would think and to understand how our thinking can overcome any tricks and schemes that the enemy may have for us. You must believe the words in Scripture so definitively that you believe them to be your own. God's mental armor is the most powerful armor that you can utilize in your marriage/relationship. In times of conflict or discord, believing the Word of God and filing yourself with thoughts of love, forgiveness, and peace can begin to take you mentally to a place that enables you to manifest these very things in your marriage/relationship. The armor of love, peace, forgiveness, or joy can only be applied to one's life by applying the thoughts to one's mind in a way that affirms what God says within them. The act of loving someone, creating peace with someone, or forgiving someone, begins with the thoughts to do so. Those thoughts which are the thoughts of God Himself must connect with the soul of man/woman to manifest what is within, and outward. The best piece of armor you can take from God is His thoughts.

Think of a situation that you desire to change. Find a Scripture to support that change and study God's word (thoughts) about it. Perhaps, you are having a challenging time right now forgiving your spouse/significant other. Study God's Word on forgiveness and begin to align yourself with God's thoughts on forgiveness. Begin to profess forgiveness for your spouse/significant other daily. Train your mind to embrace the thoughts that you are feeding it as they are the thoughts of God. When you begin to believe the words that you are reading, and your thoughts begin to support your belief in what you are reading, you will soon find yourself feeling the feelings of forgiveness towards your spouse/significant other. Remember your priority is God's priority especially when it aligns with His Word. Stop accepting that you can't change the circumstances in your marriage/relationship. Stop looking to others to change or help to change your marriage/relationship. Begin with yourself, and begin with connecting to the source, which is God.

Pray

Prayer is another instrument that God has given us for us to connect with Him in a way that reminds us that we are His priority. Throughout the Bible, we see stories of prayer and reminders of the power and purpose of prayer. If you are a believer that is not utilizing the power of prayer in your life, then you are missing out on all the benefits that come with connecting with God in prayer. When you connect with God in prayer, you bring your mind and thoughts to Him. Here, He can begin to assess and correct any thoughts that may not align with living a victorious, prosperous life in Him. Prayer immediately connects us with God. *1 John 5:14-15 says, "This is the confidence we have in approaching God; that if we ask anything according to His will, He hears us. And if we know that He hears us, whatever we ask we know that we have what we asked of Him."* Many people never experience a beautiful marriage/relationship because they never ask God for what they truly want. They spend so much time focusing on what they don't want in a mate and never really focus on what they do want. They spend all their time talking to God about what they don't desire and never spend time asking God for what they would like to have in their significant other/spouse. Many people may even ask, but because they do not believe that their prayers will be answered, they experience no change. The Word of God says to "Pray in the spirit on all occasions with all kinds of prayers and requests". You determine the requests that you have. God is the listening willing ear to meet your needs, but you must first request it. If a beautiful marriage/relationship full of love and joy is what you desire, make your requests known to God. Think about love and joy and get a true visual understanding of what that looks like. Feel the feelings of love and joy daily as you wait for it to fully manifest in your marriage/relationship.

Believe

You have the power through your prayers and your belief in the prayers that you present to God to experience the very things that you have prayed for. *Mark 11:24 says, "Therefore I tell you, whatever you ask for in prayer, believe that you have received it, and it will be yours."* Many people pray and look to receive but miss the importance of believing. Earlier, we talked about believing you deserve it. Once you begin to believe you deserve it, you can begin to believe that God will do it for you. Your thoughts must align with the unwavering expectation to manifest what you have prayed to God for. Many of us never manifest because we never believe. We look at the current state of our marriage or relationship and begin to feed ourselves thoughts that will continue to support it staying in that condition. We tell ourselves, things are too bad, there is no way this can get better. When we feed ourselves these thoughts but go to God in prayer for better, our negative thoughts prevent the release of the things that we are praying for. Our negative thoughts become a blockage in the pipeline of manifestation. If you want to see, God move in your marriage/relationship, ensure that your thoughts are thoughts that support your belief in the things that you have prayed for with expectancy. My husband and I had been facing financial problems early in our marriage for years. We had many moments where we felt hopeless and began to believe that things could not get better. We began to accept this condition in our life and didn't fight against it any longer. Then one-day, God spoke to my husband and informed him that if he wanted things to change for us financially, that we must first believe that God can do it. My husband and I began to feed ourselves with scriptures that increased our belief in God's ability. We began to reflect on times that God had come through for us in impossible ways all because we believed that He would. As we began to shift our mindsets around what God could do about our finances, doors and opportunities began to open and our financial situation began to improve. God showed us that it wasn't His inability to deliver that was preventing our blessing, but our unbelieving thoughts that would not allow the blessing to manifest in our life. Believing is a gift given to all believers of God. It is the very thing that confirms our connection to God. Belief is a muscle that must be worked in your life and must be fed by your thoughts. We believe that your marriage/relationship is only as bad or as good as you believe it to be. I believe I have a wonderful, blessed, exciting, committed, joyful marriage. I believe it to the core of who I am that no one can convince me differently. I thank God for the marriage that I have, and my thoughts support the marriage that I am blessed to manifest and live daily. If you want what you have visualized and prayed for, you must learn to wrap your thoughts in an unwavering belief in what you have imagined or desire.

Belief Affirmations
I Believe That I Have Received All That I Have Prayed For
I Believe God in All Things
I Believe God Daily and Trust in Him

God Equals Perfect Peace

I have had the pleasure of meeting some great people in my life. I can recall a couple that my husband and I admired a lot. They were an older couple and seemed to radiate joy and peace every time you encountered them. They lived a great life. Raised kids, enjoyed grandkids and lived their dreams, but within their marital union was a sense of peace that could only be created and rooted by their relationship with God. The Word of God says, *"You keep him in perfect peace whose mind is stayed on You, because he trusts in You" (Isaiah 26:3).* Your peace is attached to your thoughts. To keep your thoughts closely aligned with God's thoughts, you must keep your mind connected to God and the things of God. You can't feed yourself worldly relationship advice and then wonder why your marriage/relationship is failing. You can't watch toxic relationships play out on television or social media and believe that it has no impact on your mindset and thinking. Whatever you desire in your marriage/relationship, you have the power to create with your thoughts. Peaceful thoughts not only impact you or your marriage/relationship, but it also impacts the community around you. I don't know anyone who just desires to live in constant chaos, distress, or conflict. Most, if not all people desire peace whether they have it or not. Peace allows you to enjoy the union that you are in with your spouse/significant other. It allows you to go through the challenges of life centered in peaceful thoughts created by God.

To experience the marriage/relationship that you desire, your dominant thoughts must be thoughts of peace. When you feed yourself negative thoughts or thoughts of conflict or distress, you begin to live those things out in your marriage/relationship. Have you ever known a couple that all they ever do is fight and argue? This couple has created the atmosphere of conflict and strife by the thoughts that they have daily concerning their marriage/relationship. If we could read their thoughts, we would surely find thoughts like, "All we ever do is argue", "She better not start with me today", "I just want one day without arguing with him". Their thoughts are the very thing that invites and create chaos and conflict in their lives. Because they are focusing on everything concerning conflict, they begin to manifest in their lives the very thing that they mostly think about. If you are facing conflict and chaos in your marriage/relationship, you must begin to feed yourself thoughts of peace concerning it, even when the environment is chaotic. You must create peace in your mind so that the peace can begin to manifest in your life. As believers, we understand that everything began with a thought, and God created the universe through what His thoughts were. You have the same power within you to create from your thoughts. The spirit within you wants to create peace in your life and marriage/relationship as it is a fruit of the very Spirit that resides within you. You determine your peace. Begin to imagine peace within your marriage/relationship. Write out affirmations concerning peace in your life so that you can begin to shift the thoughts that you are having in your marriage/relationship. Some great affirmations, to begin with, are below. Begin to read them morning and night for 30 days. Believe that you have received this peace and believe with expectancy. God wants to deliver your desires to you because you are the priority of God.

Peace Affirmations
I Am Surrounded by The Spirit of Peace
I Am Peaceful
My Marriage/Relationship Has an Abundance of Peace Flowing Within It

Chapter Eight
The Mental Choice-To Live or Die

Very early on in life, we learn about the power of words. Before we ever hear or learn the Scripture, "There is life and death in the power of the tongue," experience teaches us this concept. As a child, someone may say something cruel that just shatters your confidence to the point that tears run down your face. A parent can uplift your spirit and mood with love and encouragement spoken from their lips. Our words have and always will have life and death power. Many of us never make the connection of our words to our thoughts. Some people believe that what they say has nothing to do with what they think. This is a flawed and untrue belief. **Our thoughts are always tied to the words that we speak. Whether we are conscious of the thought that drives the words or not, they are always driven by our thoughts.** That is why the surest way to know what someone thinks about you is to watch and pay attention to what they say about you. **If the power of life and death is in the power of the tongue and our words are driven by our thoughts, then the ultimate power lies in the thoughts that we have before we ever really speak them.**

Take for instance, a person that only ever speaks negatively or pessimistically. If you interact with people in the world, you are sure to know a few and may even have some as friends or family. Many of us realize that they tend to only speak negatively about life. Their words are constantly full of death. But where do these negative words stem from? Of course, they do not just magically come out of their mouths with no internal connection. At the core of their thought process and dominant thoughts, are negativity and ill thinking. This person is sure to have negative thoughts daily, consciously and subconsciously. They have surely trained their mind to embrace all negative thoughts, negative energy, and negative images that continue to feed and reinforce this negative mindset. Their words are simply a reflection of their constant thoughts. **Before there is ever a choice to speak life or death, there is a choice to think it. Your words are only a reflection of your thoughts and only help to manifest what you have already imagined with your thoughts.** Couples who speak of joy, peace, love, kindness, goodness, forgiveness and unity are supported by the thoughts that they have internally before their words are ever spoken externally. Their dominant thoughts are full of life and love, so they create an atmosphere of life and love within their marriage/relationship. Your words are a wonderful way to assess your thoughts about your marriage/relationship, as well as the thoughts about your spouse/significant other.

You have the power to create what you desire to see in your marriage or relationship. God will not do the work for you. You have the power to do it. When you exercise this great creative power God gave you, it will change the experiences that you have in your marriage or relationship. It may seem crazy at first, but everything begins with a thought that is then spoken into existence. That is how God created the world. He said let there be light, and there was light. That is how inventors who created the airplane, automobile, iPhone, spaceship all began. They spoke it into existence first before anything was ever created.

I can recall a time in my marriage where I felt that my husband was acting very selfishly, especially during intimate moments. I had resolved in my mind that he was selfish by the thoughts that I had begun to constantly feed myself. Now, don't mistake me, he had one or two selfish occasions that were very real. The problem was that, I had taken these two occasions and now used them to solidify my thought process around his selfishness when there were thousands of other occasions that proved he was unselfish. I had decided to focus on what I hated that he did minimally, more than what I loved that he did, majority of the time. In marriage/relationships, we tend to do this a lot and aren't always consciously aware that we are doing it. Not too long after thinking about how selfish he was, did an argument surface where I yelled out to him that "you are so selfish". I even took it a step further and said that he is always selfish and has always been selfish. Although my words did not line up with the evidence of unselfishness within our marriage, my thoughts had justified and guided my words in a manner that I now so ardently believed them. I believed the thoughts of death that I began to speak it into my marriage and if I weren't careful, would have begun to create the very thing that I thought. As we understand the power that our thoughts have on the words that we speak, we must be careful paying attention to and being diligent about what we focus on. What you focus on, you magnify.

Focus is Important

Our thoughts that can become words are fed by our focus. What we focus on becomes the primary food for our thoughts. That is why it is important to filter what you watch, what you read, and what you listen to - what you are taking in has your absolute focus. It is also important to focus less on the bad in your marriage/relationship and more on the good within it. When you focus on the good things, you begin to generate good thoughts that drive the words that you speak into it. It is very difficult to speak ill of a marriage/relationship that you have abundant good thoughts about. It is difficult to tear down a spouse that you have abundant positive, loving thoughts for. What you focus on in your marriage or relationship is absolutely what your words will speak. I can always tell the thoughts that are consuming a couple that we are coaching by listening to the words that they speak about each other or their marriage/relationship. It is always clear what the focus is by the words that are spoken. To think your marriage strong, you must be diligent and aware of what you give your focus to. You must give your focus to positive things within your marriage/relationship even when some negative behaviors and traits may be present within them. This does not mean that you don't discuss and address behaviors that are toxic within the marriage/relationship, but it does mean that you cannot focus on them for life. You must address them and move on, and bring back your focus to the goodness and blessings within your marriage. Your thoughts are connected to the things that you focus on. Couples who take the time to read books that strengthen marriage/relationships, to watch movies that reflect love and joy, or surround themselves with other couples who are happy and joyful, typically begin to have thoughts of love and joy. Your focus feeds your future. If you desire to change the state of your marriage/relationship, change your focus. As your focus begins to change and your thoughts begin to change, you will notice that your words are changing as well. You will begin to hear more words of life and less words of death within your marriage/relationship. Make every effort to focus your thoughts on the things that you desire to see manifest in your life.

Forward Thinking

A sure way to ensure that the mental choice you have made for your marriage/relationship is one of life, would be in focusing your mind forward. One of the best-known Scriptures of today was written by the great Paul who said, "I am forgetting those things which are behind and reaching forward to those things which are ahead". This is what forward-thinking looks like and what it means. Your thoughts should always be on what you desire to have even if it is not your present circumstance. When you intentionally guide your thoughts forward, you establish hope within your thoughts and your marriage/relationship. Paul understood that there was no benefit in looking to the past. That to move forward, you had to look forward, and when you look forward, you guide your thoughts in a forward-thinking way. Most people who look to the future more than they look to the past have a mental choice of life working within them. Their thoughts are full of possibility and positivity for the future no matter what past circumstances may have been. Forward thinking people are people that experience the best in their marriage/relationship because they expect the best to happen for them in the future. They do not let their current circumstance dictate their outlook on life or their marriage/relationship. They understand the power in their thoughts and that their present thoughts create the future that they expect to live and have. To effectively think your marriage/relationship strong, you must be able to think forward and forget the past. You must be able to silence the past thoughts that want to steal your current joy, hope, or peace. You must be able to remove yourself from the past feelings of hurt, pain, and disappointment and replace them with feelings of prosperity, love, enjoyment, and excitement. Forward-thinking begins with thoughts of moving forward. It is an expectation that what is ahead of you is so much better than what is behind you even if what is behind you was great.

As we progress through life, our experiences begin to attack our natural nature of thinking forward. If you can recall back to your youthful years, everything you imagined for yourself moving forward was full of positivity and possibility. We typically felt as if the world was ours to conquer. Somewhere through the process of becoming adults and facing challenges, we began to adopt a limiting mindset that encourages past thinking and reflecting on current circumstances. God did not design us to move backward or remain stagnate. He did not design our minds to stop producing thoughts that would move us forward in life no matter what our circumstances looked like. Many marriages/relationships that find themselves stagnated have moved away from forward thinking and have begun to feed themselves thoughts of lack and limitation. Remember you can move your marriage/relationship forward no matter what it has faced or is facing. It all begins with the thoughts that you choose to accept and let manifest in your life. Forward thinking will always help to move your marriage/relationship forward and move it forward with life beaming at the foundation of it all. After reading this chapter, take some time to reflect on your thoughts. Identify any thoughts that may be created by past circumstances or present ones, and begin to write down the thoughts that you would like to have to drive your marriage/relationship forward.

Renewing to Live

As you take the time to focus your thoughts and utilize forward-thinking, you must understand that to maintain the mental choice of life, you must renew your mind. There is no way to renew your thoughts consistently if you are not working diligently to renew your mind. The Word of God tells us, "Do not be conformed to this world, but be transformed by the renewal of your mind, that by testing you may discern what is the will of God, what is good and acceptable and perfect" (Romans 12:2). Your marriage can fully be transformed, but it will begin with the renewal of your mind. George Bernard Shaw said, "that progress is impossible without change, and those who cannot change their minds cannot change anything." Renewing your mind won't be easy; it will be challenging as many of us naturally go back to old habits that are familiar and comfortable to us rather than sticking things through for a change. But it is possible for you to renew your mind first, by renewing your thoughts daily. Make a list of daily affirmations you would like to begin to believe and think about daily. Make sure that they are positive and are written in presentence as if you already have these things. Read over them morning and night for at least, 30 days, so that they become so ingrained in your mind and heart. Place the list somewhere that is visible to you so that you can be reminded of the commitment that you have made to renew your mind. Encourage your partner to do it with you and support each other as you both work to experience the marriage/relationship that you both desire, simply by renewing your thoughts which aid in renewing your mind.

We all have adopted toxic thoughts that must be extracted from our minds and replaced with healthy whole thoughts. We make it a habit to renew our minds periodically to ensure that the thoughts that we desire to have, we are having, even when we may not be aware of our thoughts. Once you begin to manifest the marriage/relationship that you desire from renewing your mind, you will work to continue to renew your mind as often as possible. If you are reading this book, you have begun the process of renewing your mind. You now understand that your thoughts are not harmless, but very impactful in your life and your marriage/relationship. We hope that you have begun to challenge your thoughts in a way that has revealed some areas that need to be discarded or changed. Resist conforming back to your old ways or conforming to the ways of the world. The world has taught us that our marriage/relationship suffers from the outside-in instead of the inside-out. The world doesn't teach us that our thoughts are the reason so many of us are not experiencing or living the marriage/relationship that we desire. Resist the urge to turn back to mundane toxic thinking and encourage yourself to renew your mind constantly to experience the life you desire. The marriage/relationship you desire is already yours. It already belongs to you. You must now begin to release it, by ensuring that the thoughts you have align with the mental choice of life that you desire.

Chapter Nine
You Have Not Because You Ask Not

Coaching couples has given us great insight into the minds of those in relationships and marriages. We have learned that many couples, when asked what they desire in their marriage/relationship, that they currently do not have, struggle to put into words what they want. Many people are in relationships or marriages unable to fully articulate or understand what it is that they desire. If you do not know what you truly want, how can you ask for it from your spouse/significant other or most importantly, from God? The Word of God says that you do not have because you do not ask. Others, who believe in the laws of the universe, understand that receiving first begins with a simple request. Whatever your beliefs are, we all know that to manifest or receive anything in life, you must first ask. Making your request known is the beginning process towards manifesting what you desire in your life.

Perhaps, the marriage/relationship that you desire has not been attained because you have never asked for it. Perhaps, your thoughts have never held the possibility of experiencing the very thing you desire, so you never fix your lips to ask God for it. We know that God knows our thoughts, but some of us have rested on this knowledge and have refused to ask God for what we deem He already knows. God is a respectful God. He will not just intrude on your life and create for you what you do not ask Him to create in your life. If you desire more love, ask for more love. If you desire more joy, peace, understanding, patience, forgiveness, wellness, or prosperity in your marriage or relationship, you must first ask for the very things that you desire. As discussed earlier in the book, our inability to ask is directly tied to our feelings of unworthiness. When you feel unworthy of anything, you cannot and will not ask for it in your life because you truly do not feel that you deserve it. We are here to inform you that you are worthy of experiencing and feeling all the love, joy, and peace that God has created to exist in our lives and in our marriage and relationships.

Think about someone that you love. Think about them struggling in life and struggling silently. None of us would want someone we love to struggle or suffer in silence. We would do all that we could do for them if only we would have known that they were struggling. Once they decide to ask for help in whatever they may have been struggling with, we naturally say yes to help them and do all that we can, to reach the outcome they desire. This is what God wants to do for you when you simply ask. The answer to your request is YES! Yes, to a better marriage or relationship. Yes, to Love. Yes, to Peace. Yes, to Prosperity. Yes, to Kindness. Yes, to Friendship. Yes, to Joy. Your yes is not avoiding or fleeing from you; it is there waiting for you to ask - waiting for you to turn the light to green and give it a go into manifestation. The Word of God in John 14:13-14 says, "Whatever you ask in My name, that will I do, so that the Father may be glorified in the Son". God expects us to first ask. **Asking is a gift that many of us never unwrap out of fear that what we ask will never be received. We believe that we avoid hurt and disappoint by not asking, but the real disappointment is felt by those who have the desire to ask, but fear holds them captive from asking.** Your power begins in your asking.

Ask from Your Belief, Not the Belief of Others

As a mother, I am often entertained when one of my boys sends the other to ask for something that they both may want. For instance, they may desire a snack or to go outside, and they will decide which of them will ask based upon who they perceive will receive the yes. When we go through life, we often begin to shift what we ask based on what we have seen others acquire from asking, or we go to others to ask through them for something that we have direct access to God to ask for. When you desire something in your life, do not look around you to see if others have been able to receive what you desire, before you ask. What you believe you can have does not have to be validated by others in your life receiving it as well. Neither is your yes contingent upon who asks it for you. You have the power to receive your yes for you. Just ask. Our generation today looks to everyone first to ask for things. If we want to start a business, we ask friends and family what they think about our business idea. In a sense, we are asking them if we can do it. We are asking them to give us permission to create something that they have no vision for. Those of us in a difficult relationship or struggling through life may ask a counselor, therapist or coach if it is possible for us to heal, to have a healthy marriage or relationship, or even to experience a better life. While these people and their crafts are great, our ultimate desires should only be taken to God, and our belief that we can receive it is a partner with yes to help it manifest in our lives. God is the only one with the approving power to assist you in creating the very thing that you desire to see in your life or your marriage/relationship. Jesus said, "as you believe so shall it be done to you". How powerful and affirming is that. You can receive what you believe you can receive. If you want to truly experience joy, peace, and love you can experience it by what you believe. You must guide your thoughts in an affirmative way that what you think you can have, you already have, and soon you will see it manifest in your marriage or relationship. Also, if you believe that your marriage or relationship is over, bad, or challenging you will also receive this in your life as well. Whether what you believe is good or bad, it will manifest in your marriage or relationship because you will always receive what you believe. The great Napoleon Hill said, "whatever the mind can conceive and believe the mind can achieve." Imagine the possibilities of growth and prosperity that your marriage or relationship has yet to experience. See yourself experiencing these beautiful things day and night and begin to believe them within your heart. Paint the image of success, wholeness, and abundance in your mind and place your marriage or relationship in the center of it all. Feel like you have it before you have it. Exercise your faith in a way that creates your desires, so that you can begin to live it out on earth as it is in Heaven.

The Closer You Feel to God the Easier It Is to Ask and Believe

When I was a child, I can recall asking my parents for any and everything. There would be things I would see on a commercial and instantly, I would ask if I could have that very thing. I never had a thought not to ask for something from them because the relationship that I had with my parents was a close one where I trusted the love they had for me, so I felt comfortable in asking for anything I desired. This isn't to say that the question was always met with a yes; in fact, I heard no many times. The point I am making here is that when you have a relationship with someone that is classified as a provider for you and loves you, you feel comfortable asking for anything from them. This is the relationship that God desires us to have with him. He desires us to just ask without fear, judgment, or doubt. When you have a true relationship with God, you understand His nature of love, kindness, and will towards you, that you freely feel comfortable in asking Him for your desires. Most of us who struggle with asking God for anything, have not fully connected with God as His children. Any child that feels loved and connected to a parent will ask for anything from that parent because they understand the parents love and desire to meet their needs and wants. When you understand God's true nature and desire to honor your requests, you begin to not just ask for materialistic things, but things that truly bring joy, peace, and love in your life. You begin to align yourself with the spirit of God and begin to ask for the things that will lead to your ultimate growth and development in a way that not only benefits you but benefits the world around you. You are the only thing holding you back from experiencing the phenomenal marriage/relationship that you desire. Your inability to ask is your inability to access what God has already stored up for you. The marriage/relationship that you desire is available to you only if you choose to ask. Asking is the most freeing experience you can have. We have learned to ask for everything that we desire to have in our marriage and in our lives. People will tell you that you cannot have a marriage full of happiness and joy all the time. That is a lie. You can have it. You just first must ask, believe and receive it for yourself. When you believe that no marriage/relationship can maintain fidelity, then you are never able to experience it for yourself, because your belief in the inability to experience it halts your action of asking for it. To ensure that you can ask for anything from God, you must not take on limiting beliefs that prevent you from asking what is possible. Your beliefs should be tied to your relationship with God. When you have a relationship with God, you understand that the joy and love you can experience is limitless, when obtained through asking God.

Your Anxiety is Tied to Your Inability to Ask and Believe

Philippians 4:6 tell us to "be anxious for nothing, but in everything by prayer and supplication with thanksgiving let our requests be made known to God." Simply put, instead of worrying about something that you want or desire, simply ask and believe it, while thanking God for answering your request. Anytime anxiety is present in your life, you have either not asked for something that you desire from God, or you do not believe that you can receive what you desire from God. Those who ask in confidence of God do not experience anxiety because they believe God for the yes and have already thanked Him for the manifestation of what they have asked and believed. Anxiety is always created from a place of doubt. Where there is no doubt, there is no anxiety. Where there is anxiety, doubt, and its counterpart, fear are present and dominate the feelings at the time. Anxiety is like a barrier to manifesting your desires. Many of us in marriage and relationships are operating daily from a place of anxiousness, that is preventing us from experiencing and manifesting the marriage/relationship that we ultimately desire. **You cannot believe that God answers prayers or your requests and still worry about Him not answering the prayers or requests at the same time.** Doing so is ridiculous. You either ask and believe, or do not ask and do not believe. To ask and not believe is a waste of time and energy, for you cannot manifest what you truly do not believe you can have. In Matthew 7: 7-11 it says, "Ask, and it will be given to you; seek, and you will find; knock, and it will be opened to you. For everyone who asks receives, and he who seeks finds, and to him who knocks it will be opened. Or what man is there among you who, when his son asks for a loaf, will give him a stone?" This is a straightforward way of saying ask for what you desire, believe that it will be given to you, and it will be given to you. In God, everyone who asks receives. I know you have not been taught this. I know that religion has taught you that you must be worthy to receive, but the Word of God says "everyone who asks, receives". The issue with receiving is not with God releasing, but with us believing in the release. Religion, unfortunately, creates levels of anxiety within its believers because we are always trying to assess if we are in good standing with God, or if we are worthy of blessings from God. We begin to self-sabotage the ability to manifest from God because we deem ourselves unworthy and, in our unworthiness, we become anxious about everything and can't align our spirit with the spirit of God to manifest our desires. Understand that God doesn't need to be convinced that you are worthy; He created you as a worthy being. You are worthy! You must only kill the anxiety, created by doubt and fear that convinces you that you are not.

What You Ask is Received in Due Time

Time is one of those things that many of us feel we don't have enough of, but when we are expecting something, there is too much of it before we receive it. That thing I speak of is time. Between asking and receiving is this thing called "due time", that many of us give up in or become discouraged by. It says in 1 Samuel 1:20, "It came about in due time, after Hannah had conceived, that she gave birth to a son; and she named him Samuel, saying, "Because I have asked him of the LORD." Just like Hannah, we all must experience due time. The amazing thing about due time is that it is never the same for anyone or anything. What may take one person a year to manifest may take someone else three years to manifest. Even in things that we assume should take a certain amount of time to manifest, God has shown us that it could be manifested in a shorter period than expected. For instance, many of us understand that the ideal or expected time for a woman to give birth is between 36-40 weeks for doctors to consider a child full term and healthy. But there are many stories, that we interpret as miraculous where babies are born weeks or months prior to this time frame and are perfectly healthy and strong. Due time perhaps is something that is created by our level of asking, believing, and receiving. Due time is flexible and is dependent upon your alignment with receiving not with God's release of what you have asked. **Do not lose your belief or expectancy in the due time.** It may take time, but it will manifest right on time. The Word of God says *in 2 Peter 3:9 - The Lord is* *not slow in keeping His promises as some understand slowness".* What you consider a long time is not time at all to God. What you must understand is that if God promised it and you can see and believe for it, you can have it. His Word does not, nor cannot return void. So many times, we teach couples how to get back on track in their marriage or relationship by changing their thoughts and beliefs, but they never manifest change, because they get discouraged and anxious in the due time. What you ask for in your marriage/relationship is changed once you ask, but you can block the manifestation of the change by your thoughts and disbelief in the due time season. We must learn to embrace these words, *"In the morning, O LORD, you will hear my voice; In the morning, I will order my prayer to you and eagerly watch. (Psalm 5:3)."* We must learn to ask and eagerly watch in the due times for manifestation to occur. To eagerly watch means to watch with expectancy. Where there is expectancy, there is no doubt about receiving. When you expect to receive what you had asked for in your marriage or relationship, you can get through any due time without anxiety or doubt because you know that it was already manifested when you asked. To think it strong, you must embrace the due season with expectancy and praise. *1 John 5:14-15 says, "This is the confidence which we have before Him, that, if we ask anything according to His will, He hears us. And if we know that He hears us in whatever we ask, we know that we have the requests which we have asked from Him."* Simply put, believe without a doubt no matter the time it takes to manifest change in your marriage/relationship, believe that the change has occurred, and it will occur. Thinking your marriage strong has no time frame but if you are utilizing the skills we have talked about correctly, change should be progressive things that you see traces of as you continue to change your thoughts.

Chapter Ten
God's Wisdom Vs. Your Wisdom

Many of us go through our lives and our marriage/relationship never seeking or understanding how limited our thoughts are. We do not realize that the creator which is God has created us in a way that requires us to connect with Him so that our wisdom will begin to align with His wisdom, and our thoughts become more powerful in our lives and the lives of others. The wisdom of God is the wisdom that created the heavens and the earth. It is the wisdom that created the universe and any universal law that exists; it is all truth. What has been intriguing most to us is that as believers in God, we have an all-access pass to gaining and tapping into this limitless wisdom, that is God. We have learned that **our wisdom is nothing compared to God's in our marriage/relationship.** In *1 Corinthians 1:25 it says, "For the foolishness of God is wiser than human wisdom, and the weakness of God is stronger than human strength."* With this understanding, it is insane to believe that you can transform your marriage/relationship into something strong, without transforming your thoughts in a way that begin to align with the thoughts of God. This helps us to understand that no matter what we think about our marriage or relationship, there is always a wiser thought concerning it held within the mind and spirit of God. These thoughts have transformational power when you begin to have them, and they set you on a path of wisdom that you could not attain on your own. Some of us believe that our wisdom is the greatest wisdom alive. Although our lives are reflective of a flawed thought process, many of us never seek God or turn to Him to gain the wisdom and knowledge that we need to thrive in a marriage or a relationship. Many times, we find husbands that know it all, girlfriends that hold all the wisdom, but both are in a failing relationship/marriage because their wisdom has made a fool of them. *Jeremiah 10:21 says, "For the shepherds have become stupid and have not sought the LORD; Therefore, they have not prospered, and all their flock is scattered."* Your unwillingness to seek God and renew your mind with God's thoughts has caused your marriage/relationship to suffer in ways that you cannot understand. Suffering is not something that you should always embrace and honor in your marriage/relationship. Suffering, many times is a sign that you are out of alignment with God, and a sure sign that the thoughts that you are having are negatively impacting the life that you desire. If you want to begin to experience a strong marriage or relationship, you must begin to accept your limited wisdom, while seeking the infinite wisdom of God.

How Knowing it All Has You Knowing Nothing

We were coaching a couple who was struggling in their marriage. They were having a huge issue communicating effectively, and we were working with them to help in that area. While the wife knew that their marriage was struggling in communication, she did not own any responsibility in the communication being broken. In fact, she insisted that she had excellent communication skills and that she was not the problem at all. What she had not realized was that she was equally killing the communication in the marriage and could have possibly been more toxic to it than her husband. Her absoluteness in her ability to communicate effectively produced more negative thoughts about her husband's inability to communicate which was aiding in destroying the marriage. *Isaiah 29:14 says, "I will destroy the wisdom of the wise; the intelligence of the intelligent I will frustrate."* Here was a clear example of this scripture in action. In her effort to appear to be so wise, God was destroying her wisdom by not allowing her to be in a marriage with effective communication because her thoughts were creating a negative energy and space for ineffective communication to manifest. Her unwillingness to see the growth needed within herself, allowed her to create negative thoughts about her husband's communication skills, that worked in creating the very thing she detested in her marriage. **You have creative power within you, and that creative power manifests through the thoughts that you have.** Whether your thoughts are the wise thoughts of God or the foolish thoughts of man, they all have the creative power to manifest in your marriage or relationship. Anytime you presume to know it all, you create what you know, even if what you know has the potential to create something that you hate. Many people spend so much time and energy thinking about what they do not want or like in their marriage or relationship that it becomes their dominant thoughts, and becomes what they believe is true. God knew that our thoughts would naturally be focused on the ill's or negative things in life. His infinite wisdom led Him to birth Scripture in Philippians that says, *"Finally, brothers and sisters, whatever is true, whatever is noble, whatever is right, whatever is pure, whatever is lovely, whatever is admirable--if anything is excellent or praiseworthy--think about such things."* This is what God's wisdom is all about. Here, if we apply what is written, we will naturally move away from focusing on things that are negative, to things that are positive and good in our marriage or relationship. That focus will begin to birth numerous thoughts that begin to create and manifest the life we desire to have with our spouse/significant other. Never let your wisdom stop you from changing any negative thoughts that you may have about your spouse or significant other. If you are willing to let the Spirit of God override your wisdom, especially in its negativity, you can begin to create a stronger marriage/relationship.

Stop Leaning to Your Own Understanding

"Trust in the Lord with all your heart, and do not lean on your own understanding. In all your ways acknowledge Him and He will direct your path" (Proverbs 3:5-6). There is nothing more assuring to a believer than this Scripture here. It is a wonderful feeling to know that our trust in God and God's wisdom will lead us down a path directed by Him. Down a path of goodness and blessings. Down a path of peace, joy, and

love. When you begin to lean on the thoughts that are in God, you begin to experience all the goodness that God has for you to experience. Your thoughts begin to create and attract the very things that you believe about your marriage/relationship. There is no way to lean on the thoughts of God and not experience the beauty of God in your marriage/relationship.

We must understand that any and every thought that you need to have to repair, heal, and improve your marriage/relationship is within the spirit and thoughts of God. The Word of God says, *"but if any of you lacks wisdom, let him ask of God, who gives to all generously and without reproach, and it will be given to him" (James 1:5)*. When you begin to ask Him for wisdom concerning your marriage/relationship and open your thoughts to being transformed by the thoughts of God, you will begin to obtain the thoughts that you need to live the marriage/relationship that you desire. When you turn to God and connect with God, He will never release negative thoughts into your mind. God is a God of love, joy, peace, and forgiveness. His very essence is one of positive, uplifting, beautiful and harmonious thoughts. When you find yourself struggling to generate good thoughts within your marriage or relationship, more than likely, you are no longer connected to the thoughts of God, but you are connected to your own understanding. You are connected to your physical and present experiences and feelings, instead of the promises of God. For many of us, it is hard to detach what we are currently facing or dealing with, from what we believe God can do. Many of us discount the ability of God, bringing our positive thoughts to life, especially when our negative experiences are existing daily in our marriage or relationship. To think your marriage or relationship strong is no different than thinking healing for someone who is presently ill. You may see this person battling against cancer. Every day that you see them, they may look and feel worse and worse, but you stand in your thoughts of healing, believing that God can change their situation at any moment and they can be healed. This is what is required of you to transform your marriage or relationship and make it stronger. You cannot lean to your understanding of what feels real and concrete and definite right now to you in your marriage or relationship. No. You must hold on to the thoughts and desires of beautiful change and possibility that rest within the thoughts that you have in the ability of God, to generate a dissimilar experience and outcome for you very soon. *Romans 8:6 says, "to set the mind on the flesh is death, but to set the mind on the Spirit is life and peace".* You must learn how to set your mind on the spirit of what you desire in your marriage and relationship and not on the current state of it that is the flesh. When you can't see past your circumstance, you must train your mind and thoughts to override it and see past them to begin to create the marriage or relationship you desire to experience.

Chapter Eleven
Giving Is Tied to Receiving

Many of us, when we think about giving and receiving, can only perceive and understand it from a monetary perspective. We believe that if we give away our money to those in need, it will be given back to us. Many of us quote the Scripture, *"Give, and you will receive. Your gift will return to you in full--pressed down, shaken together to make room for more, running over, and poured into your lap. The amount you give will determine the amount you get back." (Luke 6:38 NLT)*. While we truly believe in this Scripture ourselves, we do not believe that it is simply about money. This Scripture can be applied to anything that you give but should mostly be applied to the thoughts that you give out. Many of us never make the connection of the giving of our thoughts to the receiving of circumstances and experiences in our lives. As we have said throughout this book, your marriage or relationship is only a reflection of the thoughts that you have about it. When you generate an abundance of negative thoughts in your mind, you receive the experience of those abundant negative thoughts in your marriage/relationship. When you create an abundance of powerful positive life thoughts, you begin to create these things for you to experience in your marriage/relationship. Norman Vincent Peale said, "if you change your thoughts you can change your world." Perhaps the thoughts that you are giving to your marriage or relationship right now is 100% of the problems that you are facing right now in it. Your negative, toxic giving is leading to your negative, toxic receiving in your marriage/relationship. What you put into anything is always what you end up getting out.

If you Want to Receive Differently, you Must Give Differently

Albert Einstein said, "to do the same thing repeatedly and expect different results is the very definition of insanity." Are you operating your thoughts from a place of insanity? Are you constantly and continually thinking the same negative things repeatedly, expecting to experience something different in your marriage or relationship, other than that which you are giving through your thoughts? If you desire to receive the experience of love, joy, peace, possibility, or happiness, they must be the very thoughts that you give yourself and your marriage/relationship, to receive them back in manifested forms. Thinking it strong is a conscious effort to change your thoughts in a way that produces and creates the very desires that you have within your marriage/relationship. If you desire an abundance of love, your thoughts must be filled with an abundance of love. Things that you love and things that make you experience love must be the dominant thoughts in your mind. You must also create thoughts of love, inclusive of your spouse/significant other. These thoughts will begin to manifest between the two of you when they are your dominant thoughts, and you believe them so passionately. So many couples become consumed in the circle of negativity within their marriage or relationship, that they never turn on the switch to change their thoughts into hopes of experiencing anything differently. We have spoken with numerous couples whose negative thoughts were so concrete and so confirmed within their minds that it acted as a barrier against any hope or possibility of experiencing something wonderful in their marriage or relationship. They had become so extremely self-convincing, that negativity was the only outcome they would experience in their union, so what they created for themselves and their union was wrapped in negativity. They simply received what they gave. There is no way to receive love by generating thoughts of hate. There is no way to receive peace by giving thoughts of discord and conflict. There is no way to receive happiness by giving thoughts of sadness and pain. Your marriage/relationship will give you what your thoughts create. While you may not perceive yourself to be able to shape and change your reality, your thoughts operate in a creator mindset regardless of the ability that you attach or detach to it. Meaning your thoughts do not need your approval to manifest in your life. While you may think that changing your thoughts is a waste of time, life is proving to you that your condition is heavily tied to your mindset. You will continue to experience that which you constantly think about but do not desire, because you will not transform your mind in understanding that your thoughts are creating your reality. The energy that you spend thinking negatively has the same creation power that thinking positively and hopefully has. Why not then, take the time and switch your thoughts and watch what can be created for you? Do not look for immediate results in the natural. Immediate results only take place in the supernatural. You must understand that once you begin to release positive life-affirming thoughts into your marriage and relationship, the change has occurred instantly, although the manifestation is not instant. You must learn how to have the same patience in building your marriage/relationship with your thoughts as you had for destroying it. If you take the time to believe in what you are changing within your marriage/relationship, you will begin to see it manifest for you.

Sow It

Giving is tied to receiving. It is also connected to the principles of sowing and reaping that we would like to discuss. To think it strong, you must first take ownership and responsibility that what you are reaping is in relation to the thoughts that you have sown into your mind and thus, into your marriage/relationship. Throughout the Bible, we hear and read about sowing and reaping. Throughout these stories, there is never a time that we learn about someone sowing grain and reaping beans or someone sowing beans and reaping corn. Just like with farming, what you plant in seed form, with your thoughts, is what you harvest in life. The thoughts that you plant in seed form in your mind about your marriage/relationship from a negative or toxic perspective, you will always harvest. *Job 4:8 says, "According to what I have seen, those who plow iniquity and those who sow trouble harvest it."* This passage confirms what we have said above. Whatever you sow in your marriage or relationship via your thoughts is what you will reap in the harvest of it. Many people may say that they have not sown the things that they are experiencing, but for you to experience or reap anything in your life to some degree, you have sown it. Whether consciously or subconsciously, the thoughts were sown and believed, creating the negative experience that you have within your marriage/relationship. The beautiful thing about sowing and reaping is that you can always change what you are sowing to experience a different outcome when it's time to reap. The seed of your thoughts does not have to be the same unless you choose to let them be so. If you truly desire a strong marriage or relationship, think it! Think it so strongly and so absolute that your thoughts have no choice but to create and manifest the marriage/relationship that you desire.

We must always remember that reaping is guaranteed although the time frame can never be absolute. *Galatians 6:9 says,* "*Let us not lose heart in doing good, for in due time we will reap if we do not grow weary.*" When you begin the journey of thinking your marriage or relationship strong, you must not lose heart in believing that the thoughts that you are constantly sowing will return you the harvest that you desire. Do not let yourself or others discourage you from trusting and believing your thoughts and their ability to positively create for you. You must believe in this process, and you must be committed to seeing it through no matter the time frame. As we look back on our own marriage, we realize that anything we ever changed in our marriage, we changed first by the thoughts that we sowed into it. If it was something regarding the love between us, how we managed or produced money, or how we raised our kids, we always initially began with a conversation on how we were currently thinking about the situation. After that, we would discuss how we needed to change our thoughts in a way that would create what we desired to see. You do not need to look outward to change the circumstance or situation of your marriage/relationship; you only need to look within. From within, we all shape the images of our thoughts and beliefs. If you are not satisfied with the effects of what you have created, it is easy to change the cause by changing the thoughts of what you are sowing.

There are Levels to Reaping

In Mark 13:8, it talks about the seed that was sown and how it returned three diverse levels of crop. One produced at 30, another at 60, and the other at 100. We must inform you that there are levels to reaping that are contingent upon your level of belief and the efforts you placed in sowing great positive seeds. When you only believe to a certain degree or level, you produce a certain level of harvest or effect for your marriage/relationship. If you begin to change your thoughts but only slightly believe that it may come to pass or only believe for certain aspects to change, you may very well only experience change regarding those things. You may only experience 30% of change because you only believed for 30% of change to occur. You may experience 60% of change in your marriage/relationship because your level of expectancy was only at a 60% level. But all of us have the capacity and the capability to change our marriage/relationship 100%, if only we believe and change our thoughts at 100%. **You must understand that thinking it strong will only work for you to the degree in which you work it. If you don't work it, it won't work for you.** You can create 100% of the marriage or relationship that you desire. Each day, you must work to create 100% of the thoughts that will support the change and creation that you have imagined. You determine your level of change and impact.

In all, the gift of sowing and reaping has been given to you to assist you in designing and creating the life and marriage/relationship that you want. You must utilize this gift with clarity and precision. To ensure that what you sow you reap or that what you give you receive, you must always ensure that the thoughts that you produce are the same thoughts that you want to live off of, for the duration of your marriage or relationship.

Chapter Twelve
Will Your Thoughts

Every morning after getting out of bed, I have been committed to determining and creating the kind of day that I desire to have. We call it commanding our day. Some days are easier than others, as there are days where I wake up full of joy and energy, and other days where it is a little harder to fill so vibrant and joyful. On those tough days, I am quick to recall a popular Scripture that says, *"this is the day that the Lord has made, I will rejoice and be glad in it".* What has become my focus is the words of "I will" rejoice, or even simpler the words "I will". This implies to me that we have a choice to feel and think a certain way even when our emotions and feelings may not currently support the feeling. What we have learned over time is that everyone has the power to will their thoughts when those thoughts do not just come naturally. Someone that is feeling down has the power to will themselves to feel joyful and grateful. Someone who is feeling sad can will themselves into feeling happy. Someone who is feeling unloved can will themselves into feeling loved. Someone who is thinking negatively has the power to will positive thoughts. God has granted us the ability to will our thoughts from within no matter what the conditions on the outside of us are trying to draw us to feel. As you work towards strengthening your marriage or relationship, be prepared to will your thoughts when the thoughts and feelings you desire to have are not coming so naturally.

As you work to will your thoughts from a bad place to a good place or from negativity to positivity, take the time to reflect on all the things that you are grateful for and that are going right in your life. Make a mental or physical note of all the wonderful blessings that currently exist in your life, and the things that bring you absolute joy today. When I am struggling to feel the feelings of joy and peace that I desire, I quickly think about the blessings that God has given me daily. I reflect on the great health of my four boys. I reflect on the mind that God has given me to be able to create and think on another level. I reflect on the love that I can pour into my husband and the love he pours into me. There are so many things that I can find to be grateful for, and I am sure you can do the same. When you begin to reflect and become grateful for all that is working in your favor, you will begin to see that your mood gradually begins to increase towards a better place. You will begin to realize that there is no way to remain defeated, sad, discouraged, or angry and embrace gratitude at the same time. Gratitude has a consuming power when ignited into your mind and thoughts. Gratitude has the power to create an abundance of love and peace in your life.

If at First You Don't Succeed, Try and Try Again

As you move from negative thoughts to positive ones, it is easy to get discouraged and give up when we either fail to think positively, or we do not see the results fast enough. Our prayer is that you will not give up in the trying times or times of temporary failure. To think your marriage or relationship strong is an ongoing task that does not end even in the success of it.

As you begin this journey, it is done in 90-day increments. During these 90 days, you may find that there are some days in which you are filled with positive life thoughts and days where negative thoughts slip in. Do not give up. Start over and continue to try again to only focus on positive life thoughts. You must remember that it takes 21 days to form a new habit. If you desire to bring about real change in your marriage or relationship, you must continue to work at consistently bringing about that change. The more you do it, the easier it becomes. After a few weeks, you will find yourself with an abundance of positive life thoughts about your marriage and relationship. You must look at this process of renewing your mind much like that of a baby learning to walk. As babies begin to walk, they typically fall more times than we can count. Even as these babies fall, all of them continue to try to walk again. They get back up and try again. They never get discouraged and decide to give up on trying to walk. Instead, with every step that they make successfully, it seems to encourage them to want to try again for more steps. This is what the journey to renewing your mind is like. Every step towards better thoughts must be acknowledged and celebrated not to get discouraged and revert to toxic negative thinking. You must look at every failure in the process as part of the process towards mind renewal.

I can recall when I started to truly look at the thoughts that I was having and began my renewal process. Initially, it seemed to go well. I was confident that I would overcome the negative thoughts that I had allowed to become part of my life. For a few days, I was doing exceptional by my account, but then something happened. I got some unfortunate news about something one morning that set that my day on a path of negativity. After getting the news, everything seemed to go wrong for the rest of the day. Every thought that I had after that initial call was full of devastation, doubt, and negativity. By the end of the day, I was feeling so bad and heavy, and began to try and get myself out of this negative state. After reflecting on my day, I realized that I had failed in really being mindful of the thoughts that I was having. I had begun to only accept and implant negative thoughts all day because I had become negative from that one phone call, that in hindsight, wasn't as bad as I saw it to be. Everyone that works to renew their minds has good days and bad days. We all have days where we are feeling great and manufacturing great thoughts, and then, we have those days where we let life come in and alter what we want to think and feel. No matter what life throws at you, within you is the ability to truly experience and drive the kind of day you want, by feeding yourself positive life thoughts.

As you take this journey of renewal, take the time to chart your progress at each 90-day interval. As you will see, the days that you tend to fall short of the right thoughts will decrease as you master having the thoughts that you desire to have. In each interval, you will see yourself mastering this renewal process more and more. The key is never to get discouraged and to never give up. Continue daily to pay attention to your thoughts and to control the impact that any negative thoughts may have on you. You have the power to change your life and create the life you desire. Repetition is the sure way to form a habit and to truly renew your mind by changing your thoughts. Remember not to focus on your failures as you renew your mind but focus on the times that you are successful in controlling your thoughts, in a way that positively and purposefully impacts your day, and your marriage or relationship.

I recently came across something called the aggregation of marginal gains. It is something typically used from a business perspective, but the concept is that in the beginning, when you decide to take steps to change something, there is basically no difference between making a choice that is 1% better or 1% worse. In other words, what you change now, won't impact you very much today. But as time goes on, these small improvements (for instance, increasing your Godly positive life thoughts daily) or declines (continuous toxic negative thoughts) compound, and you suddenly find a very big gap between people who make slightly better decisions daily and those who don't. In other words, what you begin to do today to change your marriage/relationship may not show today or in a month, but over time, there will be a significant difference in your marriage/relationship compared to those who do not change their mindset and actions. You can do it, but you must make the decision to follow through daily even if you cannot physically see its manifestation yet.

Don't Attach Yourself to Thoughts of Offense

The surest way to get off track with willing your thoughts is to get to a place of offense. For so many of us, we become offended by things and people who had no intention of coming off offensively. If we are honest, some people live in an atmosphere of offense, in that they are constantly and consistently looking for someone to offend them so that they can choose to feel a certain way in their life. The acknowledgment of being offended creates a sense of un-accountability on their part. They begin to justify their negative thoughts, feelings or actions from a place of offense. As you are renewing your mind and willing your thoughts, you must understand that being offended is a choice that you make. No one can make that choice for you because it is always yours to own. Whenever you allow yourself to entertain negative thoughts or feelings and justify them because you feel offended, you are choosing to live in a negative place and not move forward.

This happens a lot in marriages and relationships. We take something that we don't like about our spouse and form an offensive thought to go along with it. I can recall a time my husband would leave to go to work before our family got up in the mornings. He would have to be at work by 6 a.m. and would often get up about 4 or 4:30 to get ready for work. As he got ready in the morning, I would still try to sleep and would become so irritated by him turning on the lights in the bathroom and not closing our door from the bedroom to the bathroom. I would get so offended by it that I started to plant thoughts in my head that he was intentionally doing this to somehow agitate or irritate me. It never crossed my mind that perhaps, he was so focused on getting ready for work that he sometimes forgot to close the door to prevent the light from shining into our bedroom. As time went by, he bought me a sleep mask so that if he forgot to close the door the light still would not bother me at all. I still use the sleep mask today, just because it allows me to have my eyes in total darkness no matter what is going on. As I began to utilize the mask, thoughts of how caring and sensitive my husband was to my needs began to fill my head instead of negative ones. I began to not be offended anymore by him leaving the door opened or closed even on the nights that I did not wear the sleep mask. I made the decision not to be offended because the decision was always mine to make. There is no way to renew your mind from an offensive perspective. If you desire to really will your thoughts, you must avoid the urge to feel offended from any and everything that your spouse or significant other may do that you do not like. We are all human and will do things that may agitate or irritate the other unintentionally. You must learn to give your spouse some grace and not be offended to keep your thoughts full of love and kindness towards them. As you begin to master willing your thoughts, always remember that being offended is always an option.

Choose to Have a Victorious Mindset Instead of a Victim's One

1 John 5:4 says, "For everyone born of God overcomes the world, this is the victory that has overcome the world, even our faith". 1 Corinthians 15:57 says, "but thanks be to God, He gives us the victory through our Lord Jesus Christ". Finally, John 16:33 says, "I have told you these things so that in me you may have peace. In this world, you will have trouble but take heart. I have overcome the world." These Scriptures can all be utilized to confirm that God intends for us to have a victorious mindset instead of a victim's one. Your mindset shapes the experiences that you have. Yes, things can happen in your marriage or relationship that you do not desire, but you do not have to be a victim to it. You have the power to will your thoughts. You can choose to be victorious. When you meet victorious people, they are vibrant, versatile and vigilant. To win in your marriage or relationships, you must cast down the feelings of victim-hood. You must decide to no longer see yourself as the victim in your marriage or your relationship. Stop seeing yourself as a victim to ineffective communication, to lack, to ill health, to selfishness, to lack of intimacy. You are victorious. You have the power to transform all these things by first transforming your mindset around them. God created us to live a victorious life even amid trials.

What is it within your marriage or relationship that you are playing victim to today? What have you feeling repeatedly defeated that is stealing your feelings of victory? What are you experiencing today that creates thoughts that things will never change and thoughts of hopelessness? You must remember that God has placed the power within you to overcome anything that you face in life. You must only make the decision to conquer it in your mind before you can conquer it in your life. You are victorious. You do not have to do anything to gain this victory gift, but to own it. Accept, embrace, and believe that you are victorious in anything, and God will align victory in your life.

Chapter Thirteen
Your Marriage/Relationship Is Your Creation

I have never seen an artist create a painting that they hate, then turn to tell others that it was their fault that the painting they painted was no good to them. This is much like what we do in the relationship and marriage that we are in. We enter it and begin to paint our lives out in our marriage/relationship with our thoughts. As we are painting our lives, many do not realize the power that their thoughts have in creating the marriage/relationship that they have or experience. No one creates the marriage/relationship that you desire but you. You create your reality by the thoughts that you have about it. If you don't like the picture that your thoughts have created, you can start on a new canvas with new thoughts to create the life that you desire in your marriage/relationship. *1 Corinthians 2:16 says, "we have the mind of Christ".* The creative, powerful, and transformational mind of Christ exist within you. Many of us never embrace or understand the power that God has given us to be creators of the lives we desire. You no longer have the right to point fingers at your spouse for a creation that you have partaken in. You must begin to take ownership and power over the creation, that is your marriage or relationship. Once you can comprehend the power you have in creating what you currently see, you will tap into that same understanding that you also have the power to change and improve what you currently see in your marriage or relationship. You are the creator!

Desire Life, Live Life, Embrace Life and Seek it Abundantly.

John 10:10 says, "I come that you might have life and have it more abundantly". Psalms 16:11 says, "You will make known to me the path of life; In Your presence is fullness of joy; In Your right hand, there are pleasures forever". Too many people are living, embracing, and chasing a life of lack, worry, and loss. These things manifest in the mind first. Before you ever experience lack, worry, or loss, you create it with the thoughts that you have. The Word of God is clear. He comes for abundant life. Your marriage or relationship is captured in that definition of abundant life. You must only believe it and desire it for yourself, to experience it. Abundant life means that all is well and covered in your life. It means that you have more than enough of all that you desire in your marriage or relationship. When you begin to tap into your creative power by renewing your mind, you begin to create a beautiful union between two committed people. You begin to experience within your marriage or relationship the very things that you have thought about. When those thoughts are full of love, passion, health, and abundance, that is what you experience. When those thoughts are full of doubt, fear, hopelessness, and lack you get to experience those things as well, because all of it is created from this creative power within you.

Over the course of coaching and counseling, I have never met so many defeated believers in my life. So many people complain about what they experience, and never embrace life, never live life, never seek life, and eventually stop desiring life. The fact that you are still living and breathing in your marriage or relationship does not mean that you are desiring, living, embracing, or seeking life. Some of you are just existing and accepting whatever life throws at you. God did not intend for any of us to just exist here on earth. He did not intend for us to just take what life throws at us from a place of hopelessness and defeat. The only time I accept what life throws at me is when I am intending to hit a home run on whatever is thrown. I have no shame in seeking and obtaining all that my Father has for me. Some people will try and make you feel guilty for seeking and living an abundant life in God. Dismiss them and all those toxic thoughts that accompany them. God is clear in what He has for you. The only thing stopping you is your limited beliefs and thoughts about having it. When you know you are an heir to abundance, you cannot and will not settle for anything less. You will work daily to create what God has said you can have because you know that it is yours and within your reach. Today is the day to affirm your creative power and begin to create the life, marriage, or relationship you desire. Below are some daily affirmations to get you started on the journey to owning your creative power:

I AM A Creator
I Create What I Want to Experience in My Marriage/Relationship
My Creative Power Flows from Within.
I Create Love Within My Marriage/Relationship
I Create Joy, Peace, Kindness, and Abundance in My Marriage/Relationship
I AM the Creator of All the Good I Experience in My Marriage/Relationship

Responding Vs. Reacting

As you continue to create the life that you desire in your marriage or relationship, you must learn the difference between these two things, response, and reaction. There is a difference between a response and a reaction to life. A reaction is emotionally driven. It's not calculated, and it's not thoughtful. Many times, it will lead to confusion and chaos in a marriage or relationship. However, a response is strategical and intentional. It is meant to bring understanding to your spouse or significant other around what your true disposition is. Those that can Think It Strong, in their marriage or relationship choose their words wisely because they understand the power that lies within them. *Proverbs 16:32 says, "He who is slow to anger is better than the mighty, and he who rules his spirit, than he who captures a city". "Death and life are in the power of the tongue: and they that love it shall eat the fruit thereof". Proverbs 18:21.* You eat from the very words that you speak into your marriage or relationship. The fruits you are bearing today are not something that you did not have a stake in creating. Some of you will not want to hear this, but you are a creator in the current state of your marriage or relationship. You cannot take a whole pizza, divide it in two, and now believe that one slice is not part of the whole. To some degree, whether by your thoughts, words or actions, you have participated in shaping what you love or hate in your marriage or relationship today. You can begin to change it by responding more and reacting less.

We have learned now, after more than a decade of marriage, the gift of response. Many times, Ronald and I will take some time, before addressing an issue that we may want to discuss with each other. That time we take before responding may be a few hours, a day or even a week. We are very strategic in how we present issues in our marriage, and we are careful to watch the tones we use to speak to each other. In our first book, we discussed how your tone is the wrapping paper to your words. If you want your words to be received the best way possible, package it the best way you can, to be received well. Reactions only lead people to have emotional actions. When you react instead of responding, it becomes a chain reaction in your marriage or relationship that continues to impact it, day after day, with negative, toxic thoughts. Being able to respond in your marriage or relationship allows you the time needed to evaluate the thoughts that you are having at the time. It allows you to assess if this will help or hurt the current state of your union. When you allow yourself the space to respond, your responses usually create an environment where openness, communication, and growth can be planted and grown. Being able to respond helps you in creating what you desire to see in your marriage or relationship.

Celebrate Growth

Any growth is growth and should always be celebrated within each other no matter how small or large it is. **1 Timothy 4:15** says, *"practice these things, immerse yourself in them, so that all may see your progress". ***Philippians 1:9** says, *"and it is my prayer that your love may abound more and more, with knowledge and all discernment".* These Scriptures all allude to growth. When you acknowledge growth within a person, it automatically creates good and pleasant thoughts within you. When you celebrate any growth that you see in the marriage or relationship, you set the atmosphere for more growth to occur. Simply put, the acknowledgment of growth only produces more growth to be acknowledged. It is like nourishment to a growing plant. Your acknowledgment of the growth no matter how small is like fertilizer to your spouse or significant other, and will feed them in a way that produces more growth for you to see. When you refuse to acknowledge any growth, you kill any harvest that you could have reaped. You trample on the little love, the little communication, the little trust, the little respect, the little sex, the little patience, the little intimacy until there is none present in your marriage or relationship.

Many of us have had moments where we have chosen not to acknowledge someone's growth, especially when our thoughts tell us that their growth is minimal. Most people just do not like to acknowledge small things, yet we walk a mile in steps, we swim by each stroke we take, and we dance by each move that we make. These small things lead to huge accomplishments or achievement. Small growth is only a part of a whole. To obtain the achievement of the whole, we must acknowledge the small improvements. I can recall last year when we were working with our youngest son on reading. He was in Pre-K at the time and had been learning more and more words. We started increasing the time we spent with him in reading and over time, his reading fluency significantly improved. In the beginning, he struggled a little, but every day brought about small improvements that my husband and I acknowledged, and he looked forward to being acknowledged. If he remembered a word from yesterday's reading that he got wrong the day before, he would become so excited and inform us that he remembered the word and got it right this time. He was letting us know that he did not want his small improvements to go overlooked. As we acknowledged his improvements, he worked harder and harder to improve in his reading as well. This is no different from what happens in our marriage or our relationship. We all desire to be acknowledged for our efforts even when our efforts fall a little short of the overall goal. When you are thinking your marriage or relationship strong, you allow your thoughts to generate words of support, acknowledgment, and gratitude for the small improvements that are seen within your spouse or significant other.

Pay Close Attention to Your Thoughts

"Whatever things are true, whatever things are noble, whatever things are just, whatever things are pure, whatever things are lovely, whatever things are of good report, if there is any virtue and if there is anything praiseworthy—meditate on these things". Phil 4:8.

Thinking it strong is all about creating the marriage or relationship that you desire by controlling your thoughts as discussed previously in the book. Many of us pay no attention to the thoughts we have, so those thoughts begin to attack the marriage or relationship that we desire. We pour negative thoughts into it and expect to see positive results. Your thoughts are the beginning of what you will create in your marriage or relationship. To create the marriage or relationship that you desire, you must pay close attention to what you think. Focus on having beautiful, godly, life filled thoughts and experience this in your life. If you entertain worthless thoughts, they will begin to manifest in your marriage or relationship. We are diligent about assessing every thought we take into our life from ourselves, and especially from others. If it doesn't support a life of abundance, we do not accept the thought as real or valid in our life. Period. You give power to the thoughts you have by your belief in them. Do not pay attention to thoughts that do not support the marriage or relationship that you desire to create. Thoughts have creative power. Always pay attention to them so that you can know what you are creating before it is ever created in the natural.

Choose Love, Repeatedly

1 Corinthians 16:14 says, "Do everything in love." 1 Peter 4:8 says, "Above all, love each other deeply, because love covers over a multitude of sins." 1 Corinthians 13:13 says, "And now these three remain: faith, hope and love. But the greatest of these is love." Proverbs 3:3-4 says, "Let love and faithfulness never leave you; bind them around your neck, write them on the tablet of your heart. Then you will win favor and a good name in the sight of God and man". **There is no way to think your marriage or relationship strong if love is not set on repeat.** You can create any and everything through the utilization of love. Love is a superpower in marriage, relationships and even in life. It has the power to change any environment or atmosphere it comes into. If you ignite, develop, and sustain love in your marriage or relationship, you will begin to create a beautiful picture of what the Word of God talks about love in 1 Corinthians 13:4. Those that create in love create in a limitless power because God is love, and God is all powerful. Love is not something that should be set on conditions within your marriage or relationship if you are trying to create something strong. While love is a choice that one makes, it should be a willing choice made daily and guided by thoughts of love in your mind and in your heart. Those that show genuine love to all, have an abundance of love thoughts roaming in their minds, looking for an outlet to spring forth through.

Setting love on repeat begins with setting your thoughts on love repeatedly. I have an abundant amount of love thoughts for my family, friends and just for humanity. I am very strategic and intentional about ensuring that loving thoughts are created towards my husband, in the times where that love may be blocked by negative thinking or negative emotions. As stated before in this book, you must learn to will your thoughts, when they are in a place that they cannot naturally flow positively. There will be many times in a marriage or relationship where you may be upset with your spouse or significant other, and while you love them, loving thoughts may not cross your mind. In these times, you must be alert and aware of the thoughts that you are having. You must ensure that while you may not like the situation you are in, love is still at the core of what you have.

Not long ago, we worked with a couple that was struggling with love thoughts. When we sat with them to evaluate their current state of thoughts, we found a pattern of negative, toxic unloving thoughts. Those thoughts were created by the current circumstances they were going through, and the mindset they had around not overcoming those circumstances. We challenged them to closely pay attention to the thoughts that they were having daily and write them down whenever they intentionally paid attention to their thoughts. After a week, we reviewed what they had written down in their journal, and they were shocked that it revealed, that over 90% of their thoughts concerning their marriage were negative thoughts. We asked them to take things a step further and write 10 positive thoughts down for every one negative thought they were conscious of. When we sat down to meet again, they were excited to share what they noticed and the impact that it had on them. They both noticed a decrease in their negative thoughts after two weeks, but they also noticed more love being shown in their actions between each other. When they began to counter the negative thoughts with an abundance of loving positive thoughts, they began to see a change manifest within their marriage.

Love is a powerful tool given to all creators to manifest what they desire to see in their life or within their marriage/relationship. When you think thoughts of love, you radiate that love to those around you. Love begins internally and reflects externally. Those that create abundant thoughts of love, align themselves with the abundance of God. They are truly those that are showing the God that abides within them to the world. If you desire to create a solid strong marriage or relationship, begin with intentional love thoughts. Do not let your thoughts become conditional or superficial. For the love we speak of is the agape love that embodies the love of God. This unconditional, limitless love has the power to truly transform any marriage or relationship. Once you begin to flood your mind with thoughts of abundant love, you will begin to eat the fruits of this beautiful seed for generations to come. Below are some love affirmations that will begin to drive love thoughts within your mind:

I AM Love
I AM Loving to My Spouse/Significant Other Daily
Love Is A Part of Me
I Have an Abundance of Love Within Me
I AM Responsible for Creating an Environment of Love in My Home Daily
I Love My Spouse/Significant Other Unconditionally

Chapter Fourteen
Fear, the Silent Killer to Manifestation

The Word of God says in 2 *Timothy 1:7*, *"For God has not given us a spirit of fear, but of power and love and of sound mind."* Fear is defined as an unpleasant emotion caused by the belief that someone or something is dangerous, likely to cause pain or a threat. If we are honest, we have all walked around with fear attached to us at some point in our lives. Whether that fear was around losing someone we love, losing something we love, being harmed by someone we love or harming someone we love, we have all experienced fear to some degree. But fear is simply a belief, and beliefs are simply thoughts that you have repeated, trust in or find to be true. If fear is a belief and beliefs are generated from thoughts, then you have absolute power over what you fear, simply by changing your thoughts. To truly shape the life you desire, you must be careful not to think about what you fear but instead, work towards a place where you do not fear anything. As we look at the Scripture above, it clearly communicates to us that fear is not a characteristic of God. It is not something that God gave us when He inserted His great wisdom, knowledge, and power within us. If fear is not a characteristic of God and we have God within us, why do we naturally tend to fear?

For many of us, fear begins as an infant when our parents try to shield us from dangerous things, to create a level of awareness. Instead, for many young children fear is created. Being aware is a great trait to have but being fearful is not. Many people pass down their fears to their children who in turn adopt these fears as their own. For many of us in adulthood, fear stems from a place of lack of control. Many of us fear things that we feel we should control but cannot. In our unsuccessful efforts to control things, we become fearful when that control is lost. Some people will tell you that you are not supposed to control aspects of your life and that God is the only person in control of your life. This is an untrue statement. When you understand the true nature of God and His infinite wisdom and power within you, you begin to understand that control is in fact, yours. Where many of us misunderstand control is in reference to trying to control others. In the Word, we learn that a fruit of the spirit of God is self-control, meaning that God has given you the tools to control self. It is an expectation that you learn, grow, and utilize this characteristic. Now, He did not give you the tools to control others, which many of us try to do. But God has given us control over us. That control allows us to live and create the lives we desire. This self-control is greatly tied to control of your mind, which in turn is control over your thoughts. God has given us absolute control over our minds and the things that we choose to think about and create. If you desire to see a change in your marriage or relationship, you must destroy and remove fear from your thoughts and actions. **Fear is the number one killer to manifestation.** When you allow fear into your thoughts, it begins to paralyze you and keep you stagnant from experiencing any real change.

As you begin this journey of renewing your mind, the fear of failing and not experiencing any change will cross your mind. When that happens, you must immediately prevent it from becoming the thoughts that you feed yourself again. Fear will try to rob you from renewing your mind by telling you that there is no benefit in renewing your mind and having these new abundant thoughts. Remember that this process of renewing your mind is a step by step process inclusive of falling short sometimes, in creating the right thoughts. As you stumble, do not let fear grip you and hold you, hostage, once again. When the spirit of fear begins to rise up within you, remind yourself of who you are and of the God within you. This God within you has power, love, and a sound mind that can assist in renewing your thoughts and overcoming fear.

Power Over Fear

As you begin to truly connect with the God within you, you will begin to harness the power that God has given you. That power is the true power of any believer, for it is the true power of God. When you begin to cultivate this power through your awareness of your thoughts and who you are, you will begin to overcome fears that have previously held you in bondage. These fears may be fears that have robbed you of experiencing the love and happiness that you have desired for so long. God has inserted within you an infinite power to overcome the spirit of fear. We can recall coaching a couple who had adopted a spirit of fear in their marriage. Both had been married before and experienced a difficult divorce. Both entered the marriage with a spirit of fear that their marriage would end up like their previous marriages, and they would have to go through another difficult divorce. As we drilled down with them, and the thoughts that were governing their minds and feelings, they began to see that they had indeed, embraced fear. What have you embraced that is wrapped in fear within your marriage or relationship? Perhaps you fear being hurt because you have experienced being hurt before. Perhaps you fear being cheated on because you have had your fair share of unfaithful experiences. Perhaps you struggle with trust because someone has severely broken your trust before. Whatever the fear may be around or stem from, you must work to destroy it so that you can begin to experience the wholeness and fullness of your marriage or relationship.

It is important to understand that fear robs you of experiencing a full life. It robs you of all the possibilities of joy, love, peace, and happiness. As you cultivate the God within you, realize that fear has no power other than the power that you attach to it when you acknowledge it in your life. For a long time in my life, I held on to the fear of shame that being molested had inserted into my life. For so long, I pushed the thought so far out of my mind that I never truly dealt with it. When I started to really deal with it, I was in a relationship with my now husband. As time went on, I never disclosed to him the molestation or how it impacted me until I begin to despise the limitations that this fear of being accepted and or rejected placed on me. I had lived with this fear of shame so long that it kept me in bondage and impacted experiencing a truly loving and sexual connection with my husband. As I began to heal from the shame and remove the fears attached to it, I could fully discuss things with my husband, and he embraced me with more love and acceptance than I ever imagined. **Fear is a choice.** It is not something that you have to accept or embrace in your life. It is something that you choose, especially when you do not understand the power within you to destroy it. In *Proverbs 29:25 it says, "The fear of man lays a snare(trap), but whoever trusts in the Lord is safe."* Fear does nothing but set traps for you in life to begin to have negative, toxic thoughts that prevent you from feeling the abundance and fullness of life. What traps are you festering in today? What traps have you created for yourself, by your love of fear, that have now become like home to you? Yes, some of us have embraced fear so much that we foolishly love it. We tell ourselves that it is safer not to love anyone than to be loved and possibly experience pain. We tell ourselves that all men cheat to avoid hurt or pain from infidelity. We tell ourselves that one woman is not enough because we are fearful of being vulnerable with another person. When you begin to justify your fear, you are secretly in a love affair with it. To change this pattern and behavior, you must diligently work with the power you have within you and break free of these toxic thoughts and mindset.

Psalms 34:4 says "I sought the Lord, and He answered me and delivered me from all my fears." This power of seeking and delivering is within us all. We all have the power to seek God and become delivered from any fears that we have in our lives. God does not deliver us from our fears by a miraculous unknown account, but instead, He begins to deliver us from the inside-out. He works within our hearts and minds with the power that He left within all of us as human beings. God will begin to deliver you by tapping into your innermost thoughts. Those thoughts that have kept you in bondage for so long will begin to be revealed to you, and you will have to do the work to cast them out of your heart and out of your mind for good. You will have to begin to replace those thoughts with abundant thoughts that destroy any thoughts of fear and lack in your life. God has given you the power within your thoughts to deliver yourself from fear and the limitations that fear imposes. Take responsibility for your power today. Connect to its infinite ability and begin to erase all bondage that is wrapped in fear out of your marriage or relationship.

Love Is a Cure to Fear

Love is a beautiful gift from God. All thoughts of love hold a supernatural creative power when implanted in your mind. Love is one of the characteristics that God has given unto us, and it has the absolute ability to overcome fear. *1 John 4:18 says, "There is no fear in love. But perfect love drives out fear because fear must do with punishment. For the one who fears is not made perfect in love."* This is such a powerful Scripture and thought to embrace and have. There is no fear in love. Fear and love are not synonymous, nor do they reside in the same place together. If you are ready to think your marriage or relationship strong, you must disconnect fear from love and love from fear. They can no longer remain conjoined twins in your thoughts. They must be separated immediately.

When we think about the fullness of love, we truly understand that love has no fear involved with it. The very essence of what love is can't be tied to fear nor, can it be experienced in fear. There is no way to truly be connected in love with another if there is a fear of being vulnerable. That fear will drive out any possibility of love because it will prevent you from being vulnerable enough to connect and experience love. To allow love to conquer your fears, you must deposit an abundance of love thoughts into your mind daily. You must be diligent about generating thoughts of love, especially when a thought of fear may spring up to rob you of that love. We have seen so many people miss out on experiencing love because they have allowed past fears and hurts to hold them in bondage. Instead of depositing an abundance of love thoughts, they choose to deposit doubt, mistrust, worry, anxiety, disappointment, and lack. If these thoughts become the abundant thoughts that you have, then you will find yourself moving more and more away from the love you desire in your marriage or relationship. Love conquers all is the most powerful thought that you can have in abundance, to experience a joyful and successful marriage or relationship.

Take some time to think about the thoughts that you have concerning your marriage or relationship today. Are those thoughts wrapped in an abundance of love or in an abundance of fear? If you have noticed an abundance of love, keep those thoughts flowing and work at increasing them even more. If the thoughts you are having are full of fear, begin to identify those thoughts and drill down their place of origin. Where did these thoughts begin for you? When you can pinpoint a place of origin, you can begin to change the narrative. You can begin to change what you have accepted to be true as untrue, which can begin to change the thoughts that you have around it. I can recall a dear friend of mine's that had gotten married. She had so many negative thoughts around the institution of marriage that I couldn't believe that she even entered into it. So many of her thoughts were wrapped in fear and toxic negative thoughts. As she went into the marriage, all the fearful, negative thoughts that she feeds her marriage began to manifest and play out in her life. She began to create all her fears and watched them manifest before her eyes. The fear that people change when they get married began to play out in her marriage. The fear that sex decreases in marriage began to play out in her marriage. The fear that marriage makes you lose yourself began to play out in her marriage because these were her dominant thoughts about marriage, and these were all the fears that unfortunately robbed her of the marriage she desired, which eventually ended in divorce.

You have the power to destroy any fear that is haunting your marriage or relationship by ensuring that you are mindful and attentive to the thoughts that you are having about it. If you desire more love, begin to have abundant thoughts of love. Love for your spouse, your family, for life, or anything that you can attach love to. Begin to affirm yourself as loving and being a part of a loving union. Take the time to act on love and begin to do loving things for your spouse or significant other without any expectations. When you begin to overflow with love, fear has no choice but to flow out of your overflowing cup of love.

A Sound Mind Conquers Fear

Much of what we have discussed in this chapter leads to this principle, a sound mind conquers fear. What is a sound mind? A sound mind is simply a mind that has the capacity to think, reason, and understand for itself. If you can think, reason and understand for yourself then you indeed, have a sound mind. Many people have a sound mind but never utilize this sound mind to overcome their fears. As stated earlier, fear is only a belief created by our thoughts. When you understand the power that lies in your sound mind given by God, you begin to understand the ability you have in destroying any fear in your life. *Phi-*

lippians 4:6, says *"Do not be anxious about anything, but in everything by prayer and supplication (asking humbly) with thanksgiving (praise) let your requests be made known to God".* When you utilize your sound mind in prayer, supplication, and thanksgiving, which is simply gratitude, you begin to ignite the power that a sound mind has over fear. When God created us, He created us all with a sound mind. A mind with no limitations and the ability to believe in whatever we choose to believe in. Many of our beliefs, which are simply our thoughts, have begun to place limits on the lives we experience because those beliefs are driven by fear. God did not give you the spirit of fear; you have chosen to embrace whatever you fear from an experience or someone else's experience. **Until you change your thoughts, you will always recycle your experience.** Some of us hold on to fear not from our own experiences, but the experiences of others. You may be part of a family that has never had a successful marriage, and you have watched each family member go through a hard divorce. You begin to create these fear thoughts around marriage that you begin to justify never marrying for yourself because your belief is that marriage never works out for anyone. When you adopt the experiences of others and create beliefs for yourself from them, you begin to live a life of fear that isn't challenged by your sound mind, because you are not utilizing the sound mind that God gave you. Open your creative mind today and begin to reprogram your subconscious mind with abundant thoughts of love and power.

Search for Peace

Peace is another sure way to destroy fear in our lives. When you are at peace and full of peaceful thoughts, you can fully destroy fear because fear cannot exist where peace resides. In *John 14:27 it says, "Peace I leave with you; my peace I give to you. Not as the world gives do I give to you. Let not your hearts be troubled, neither let them be afraid."* God has given us all a spirit of peace when we connect our thoughts and minds to his infinite power and wisdom. Marriages and relationships that are strong carry a level of peace within them that does not bend or submit to fear. They utilize this understanding of peace to overcome anything that attempts to steal or destroy this peace that God has left within them. You must understand that God has given you a spirit of peace as well. You must nurture and grow this peace with the abundance of peaceful thoughts daily.

As we have walked along this marital journey, we have learned more and more the importance of holding onto peace within our union. Peace is like oxygen to us, and we diligently seek it and protect it within our union. When fear attempts to seep in and challenge our peace, we come together with thoughts of peace and reminders of peace within our daily lives. We affirm to ourselves that we are peaceful, and that peace lives in and around us. We remind ourselves that fear is only a thought that we can choose to accept or deny in our lives because it is not of God, so it is not natural within us. This has not always been easy and has improved significantly after over ten years of marriage. During those years, we have had many fearful moments that were self-created, that we had to overcome. As we matured in understanding who we are in God and the God within us, we have been able to handle life and our marriage in a very peaceful way. As you begin to monitor your thoughts, you will begin to see how situations that attack your peace are only attacking it because you choose to magnify the fears created from the situation instead of the beauty that comes out of it. So many marriages and relationships that we have coached, choose to hand over their peace to the situation, instead of bringing the situation into their peace. **You have the power to demand every thought created by you to be surrounded by peace, even the most challenging ones.** Create and embrace peace for yourself and your union today.

Your mind is the greatest resource that God has given unto you. It can create that which you desire and unfortunately, that which many do not desire simply based on the creative thoughts that you have. When you can truly understand the power residing within your mind and your thoughts, you begin to live a fearless life and a fearless marriage or relationship. You begin to desire and believe that you can obtain and experience all the beautiful things that love creates in a marriage or relationship. Without the limitation of fear, you can create a broad and endless love experience for years to come. It is time for you to fight against the spirit of fear and destroy its limiting ability in your marriage or relationship. Below are some affirmations to get you started. As you begin to renew your mind, utilize the 'think it strong affirmation journal' to begin to create your own affirmations to guide and assist you in overcoming and destroying fear in your life, marriage, or relationship.

I Am Brave and Courageous
I Am Fearless
I Live A Courageous Life
I Am Powerful
I Am in A Powerful Marriage/Relationship
I Am Love
I Have A Sound Mind
I Am Peaceful
I AM Full of And Surrounded by Peace Daily
I Experience Peace Everywhere I Go
I have An Abundance of Peace in My Marriage/Relationship

Chapter Fifteen
Focus on The Good Until Good Is All You See

So many times, in our lives, we focus on things that impact us negatively. We experience pain, so we focus on that pain and experience more pain. We experience lack, so we focus on the lack and experience more lack in our lives. We become ill and focus on that illness instead of focusing on health to overcome the illness. Many people have not empowered themselves to understand that what they focus on has creative power in their lives. That creative power can happen quickly or take time depending on their belief in that power. To think it strong, you must choose not to focus on the light at the end of the tunnel, but instead, become the light through the tunnel. When dark thoughts begin to inhabit your mind, choose to focus on those thoughts that bring light to your life and situation. Those light thoughts are Godly thoughts of love, joy, peace, and abundance. In *John 8:12 it says, "Then Jesus again spoke to them, saying, "I am the light of the world; he who follows me will not walk in the darkness, but will have the light of life. Matthew 5:14-16 says, "You are the light of the world. A city set on a hill cannot be hidden; nor does anyone light a lamp and put it under a basket, but on the lamp stand, and it gives light to all who are in the house. "Let your light shine before men in such a way that they may see your good works and glorify your Father who is in Heaven".* When you begin to think it strong, you begin to understand that you have the power to change the atmosphere of your marriage or relationship immediately. You don't have to look for things to change weeks, months, or years later. You can become the change or the light that you desire in the darkness of your marriage or relationship, today. The power is yours. Stop waiting on God acting like a bystander to a fire raging in front of you. Instead, change it. Change it with your focus, and focus your thoughts in a way that brings light to the darkness before you. Your focus is your power in changing the circumstances before you. If you desire to experience an abundant marriage, a joyful relationship, or a loving union focus on those things until those things are all that you are aware of.

Currently, anytime one of our demeanor's are not what they need to be when we get home, the other person will shine their light and change the atmosphere. We won't feel attacked by the other person or start to blame them for their ill day. No, we begin to shine our light. We begin to flood each other with everything that we want to experience from and with each other until our mood changes to what is acceptable in our home. You are the light. The light is within you. If you don't like what you see and experience, shine your light on it until it changes. Not with sarcasm, not with a demeaning tone, not with an accusatory demeanor, and not with anger, but with love. When you focus your light towards your spouse with love, you shine that love on all the darkness and negativity that may have been existing around them. Your focus can change what you are seeing, especially if what you are seeing is not what you desire. We must understand that to experience what we desire, we must focus on the thing desired and not the thing undesired. For instance, if someone is ill and looking to become better and healthier, they must focus on being healthy. They must see themselves healthy and recovered from whatever illness they may be suffering from. Those that wish to heal cannot focus on being ill; they must focus on being healthy. This is the same for those that are experiencing conflict but desire peace, those experiencing hate but desire love, those experiencing poverty but desire wealth. Whatever it is that you desire must become your absolute focus even when the circumstances around you do not validate those thoughts. You must learn to focus on the good of anything until the good is all you see.

The Power of Gratitude/Praise with Focus

Gratitude can be defined as the quality of being thankful. Giving thanks and being thankful is a spiritual rather than religious principle, as many religious and nonreligious people embrace gratitude. To be thankful isn't always a natural thing for people to do, especially if they are limited in the many thoughts that bring about thankfulness. There are always reasons to be thankful even in the toughest situations, so you must learn how to focus on situations that make you feel thankful. Gratitude is again, a choice one can make in their lives and in their marriage or relationship. Where there is an abundance of grateful thoughts, there is also an abundance of grateful experiences because we understand that our thoughts create our experiences. Having an abundance of gratitude driven thoughts empower your marriage or relationship in ways that you could never imagine. Without gratitude, there is no way to think it strong.

Each morning, it has become a routine to thank God for all the things I am grateful for before exiting my bed. I begin by focusing on thoughts of gratitude. Always inclusive in these things, are the love between me and my husband. I am grateful for it daily, and I attempt to have thoughts and words that align with that gratefulness. When you share your life and space with another, it is easy to find things that irritate or annoy you, especially if you are looking for them. Many of us spend so much time together that moments of irritation may spark up. Arguments may take place, and we begin to move from thoughts of gratitude to thoughts of resentment and aggravation. It happens to us all, and no one is exempted from it. During these times, we must work to realign ourselves to a place of gratitude that can overshadow our current state of irritation. Gratitude brings us all back to thoughts of love, humility, and forgiveness. If you are working to change your marriage or relationship, insert gratitude daily. Seek things to be grateful for, daily. Show your gratitude daily towards your spouse or significant other with your actions towards them. When you are willing to be grateful, you are willing to create a circle of gratefulness within your union. You began to create an atmosphere that draws grateful experiences and situations into your life in an abundant manner. When you learn how to carry a grateful mindset, God begins to release more grateful experiences unto you and your marriage/relationship.

Praise is one of the most underutilized ways to create joy and harmony in your marriage or relationship. Out of the hundreds of strong and successful marriages that we know of, it is one of the most beneficial ways to keep your marriage healthy and strong, and to keep your mind full of positive, loving thoughts. When we praise God or praise anyone for something, it places us in a mindset of gratitude and thanks - it makes us feel good and creates beautiful thoughts within us about others and ourselves. When you feel grateful and thankful, it is hard to generate toxic, negative thoughts that can destroy your marriage or relationship. Where there is an abundance of gratitude and praise, there is an abundance of love. Think about the last time someone praised you for something that you did or simply for being the person that you are. How did it feel to be praised? For most of us, it feels great to be acknowledged and recognized. It causes us to not only feel good but also do good and find things within others around us to praise as well. Praise is a wonderful way to begin to generate thoughts that can reshape your marriage or relationship. If you desire to renew your mind and change your marriage or relationship, you must learn how to praise each other continually even in the smallest of things. The saying "when praises go up, blessings come down" is very real. When you begin to birth thoughts of gratitude and praise, it opens you up to a connection with God to receive blessings within your marriage or relationship.

We can recall a couple that we were coaching a few months back. The wife would constantly complain about her husband and the lack of love or attention that he showed her. Every time we would come together, she would focus on all the things that he did within that week that made her feel unimportant or unloved by him. After she would go through this spill, we would ask her to share with us five things that he did this week that she really loved. Each time, she could easily name five things that he did that she loved. We then asked her if she had shared any of these things with him from a place of praise or gratitude, and she said no that she had not. In this situation, the wife was choosing to only acknowledge the things that irritated her and to never acknowledge the good praiseworthy actions of her husband, although they were present. She chose only to focus on the bad until the bad was all that she saw within her marriage. When you choose to focus on the bad or challenges, instead of the good, your overall experience becomes bad or challenging. She had begun to only allow thoughts in her mind that recreated these bad and challenging experiences in her life. We began to challenge her to start her day off with praise concerning her husband. Instead of focusing on the bad, we challenged her to only look for things to praise him about and take the time to give him praise on the behaviors that she loved to see within her marriage. Within a few months, she began to see a meaningful change between her and her husband as well as a profound change in her thoughts. If you want to transform your marriage or relationship to a place of strength, you must insert praise and gratitude daily within your union.

Your Focus Creates It

As stated before, everything we focus on, we create. God has given us all creative power that begins with what we focus on. This focus drives our dominant thoughts and begins to shape our experiences and our lives. The Word of God says, "as a man thinks in his heart so is he". What you focus on and believe, you become or create in your life. So many marriages and relationships are struggling today because they do not realize that their focus is killing them daily. Many people focus their time, energy, and attention on such negative images, concepts, and ideas. Then they wonder why they begin to experience the very things that they have given their focus to. To experience and create a good marriage or relationship, your focus and thoughts must be on good and perfect things. You must be diligent in not allowing toxic thoughts or behaviors to enter your life because these things will begin to shift and change your focus.

In today's world, we are flooded with a phenomenon called reality television. While I am not solely against them, I do not participate in watching them. These programs or shows are full of negative experiences, ongoing conflicts, unsuccessful relationships, hateful behaviors, and toxic habits. Many people engage in watching these types of shows because they find it entertaining and unfortunately, so many people can relate to what they are watching. I have coached numerous couples and advised all of them to refrain from watching reality TV, for it will only have you focusing on all the things you do not desire to experience in your own life. Anything that you give your focus to has creative power in your life even if that focus is only a few hours a week. Many people can't understand why they have such conflicts in their own marriage or relationships when they engage in watching these types of shows. When you do not understand the power your mind has in creating your life, you cannot correlate your focus to your experience. You must be mindful of what you give your focus to. If you desire to have more peace in your marriage or relationship, focus on peace. Take the time out and create peaceful moments for yourself and your spouse or significant other. Go in environments that create peace within you and peaceful thoughts for you. Listen to music that makes you feel peaceful. The same goes for anything else that you desire to create. If love is on your list, do things that create a sense of love within you. Think about the things that you love and go places that you love. Consume yourself in an abundance of loving feelings and thoughts, and you will begin to create this atmosphere of love within your life.

You have the power to create the marriage or relationship that you desire by creating the thoughts that support that life. When you begin to focus on the right things instead of the wrong things, you will begin to see your marriage or relationship improve in the areas that you may have initially struggled in. Your focus must be directed at what you desire to create. Take the time to focus on gratitude and praise. As you go through your day, try to keep your focus on these things. Do not let circumstances, people, entertainment, or moods shift your focus from it. The more you keep your focus on being thankful and showing gratitude, you will begin to manifest those experiences in your life and your marriage/relationship.

Chapter Sixteen
Abundant Life in Marriage/Relationships

God desires us all to live an abundant life. That abundant life is inclusive of an abundant marriage or relationship. No one gets into a marriage or relationship hoping to experience a little good or a little love. Most people want to experience the best that they can with someone that they love. Having an abundant life within your marriage or relationship is the norm. Most people believe that struggles and conflicts are the norms in marriage and relationships, but that is untrue. So many people have conformed to the world and refuse to renew their minds to the possibilities that await them in God. God said that he came so that we may have life and have it abundantly. Your thoughts are the only things limiting you in experiencing this abundance in your marriage or relationship. Abundance is available to all that desire it and are willing to renew their minds to have it. Once you begin to create the necessary thoughts to experience an abundant life, you will be thrilled as those thoughts begin to create a life of abundance beyond your dreams. You must understand that abundance begins with an abundance of the right thoughts. You may be thinking it's impossible for you to have an abundant marriage or relationship. If this is your thought, then you absolutely will not experience it. You must tell yourself that it is possible until you believe that it is possible. In Mark 10:27, *Jesus looked at them and said, "With man it is impossible, but not with God. For all things are possible with God."* Do not count on your own strength and wisdom to make it possible. Take the time to connect with God and receive abundant thoughts from Him because all things are possible with God. The marriage you desire is possible with God. The relationship you dreamed of is possible with God. You must only begin to align your thoughts with abundance and believe that God has released that abundance to you.

An Abundance of Accountability

To experience an abundant marriage or relationship, you must have an abundance of certain things. One of those things is accountability. Those who experience an abundant marriage or relationship understand that accountability is not an option and must be utilized by both harmoniously. Each person must be accountable for their thoughts, feelings, and actions. When each spouse is accountable for themselves, it allows the other to only focus on their growth and their actions. Many couples do not experience an abundant marriage or relationship because they refuse to first be responsible for themselves. Being responsible for yourself involves being responsible for your mindset. That mindset is inclusive of the thoughts that you have daily. So many people do not want to be accountable for the things that they think, that it affects their ability to truly change anything within their lives. Being accountable for yourself is not optional in experiencing an abundant marriage or relationship; it is a necessity.

If you desire to think it strong, you must learn how to hold yourself accountable for your thoughts, actions, and behaviors. So many couples struggle when they begin to point the finger at each other and blame each other for the circumstances that they jointly face. **Where there is no accountability, there is no abundance.** Being accountable creates a level of responsibility and self-awareness that one must have if they are in control of creating the life that they desire. When you are accountable to yourself, you will assess your thoughts and actions on your own without your spouse or significant other bringing it to your attention. When you wrong them, you will address and correct the situation before they can ever bring it up as an issue. Accountability allows us all to be knowledgeable about our thoughts and actions, and to ensure that they align with the image we are creating in our marriage or relationship.

If being accountable is an area you currently struggle in, you must begin to create thoughts of accountability for yourself. You must begin to visualize yourself as an accountable person and being accountable in your marriage or relationship. When opportunities arise that call for you to be accountable, take charge and own up to what it is that you are responsible for. Begin with some affirmations that will help drive thoughts of accountability within your mind. Ask your spouse to hold you accountable in a loving way so that you may be more aware of situations that you would typically blame someone else for. Your thoughts of accountability must align with the actions of being accountable to get to a place of abundance in your marriage or relationship.

An Abundance of Priority

Wherever there is a marriage or relationship that is operating from a place of abundance, you will find a couple who takes the time to make each other a priority. There is no way to experience an abundant marriage or relationship without an abundance of making each other the priority. Marriages or relationships that are strong understand the importance of prioritizing each other daily and align their actions with their thoughts.

Out of the thirteen years of marriage and over 20 years of friendship that my husband and I have shared, we have always been at the top of each other's priority list. With everything in life, our thoughts create the behaviors that we exhibit and the experiences that we have. My thoughts are always that my husband is a priority in my life. As I fill myself with these abundant thoughts, my actions align with my thoughts in a way that demonstrates to him daily that he is a priority in my life. I take the time out to see how his day is going because he is a priority in my life. I take the time out to find out how I can make his day easier or more pleasant when he may have had a rough one because he is a priority in my life. We take the time out to prioritize each other because we understand that when we make each other a priority, we create an environment that we both are well cared for and well loved. There is no way to experience the fullness and wholeness found in an abundant marriage or relationship if you do not take the time to prioritize your spouse or significant other with your thoughts and your actions.

So, ask yourself, what are you prioritizing above your marriage or relationship? Take some time to assess the thoughts that you are having around priority and your spouse. If you feel as if you should not have to prioritize your spouse or significant other, then you can be rest assured that an abundant marriage or relationship is not ahead for you. If you are struggling in making your spouse or significant other a priority, the struggle isn't in your actions but lies in your thoughts. The more thoughts that you generate that validate your spouse or significant other as a priority in your life, the easier it will become to act on those thoughts. Remind yourself daily that your spouse or significant other is a priority and that you must prioritize them daily. Take some time to write down how you can prioritize them and think thoughts that make them a priority to you. The more you prioritize your spouse or significant other, the stronger you will become in your marriage or relationship.

An Abundance of Friendship

They say that best friends make the best partners in a marriage or a relationship. I am in total agreement with this statement as my husband, and I were great friends for four years prior to dating, and we have been best friends ever since. If you desire to have an abundant marriage or relationship, you must choose to be best friends. Yes, being best friends is a choice that you make, and you make it by creating the thoughts first about your friendship with your spouse or significant other. Those that have a strong marriage or relationship always have a strong friendship at the core of it all. They typically enjoy each other's company and prefer it over the company of anyone else.

To have an abundance in friendship, you must have friendly thoughts about and towards one another. If you have thoughts that your spouse or significant other is the enemy, then you will never form a true friendship with them. Remember thoughts become things, and your thoughts have creative power in your life. You must deposit abundant thoughts of love, friendship, trust, joy and kindness within your mind that can begin to shape what you experience with your spouse or significant other. You must create this world of friendship in your mind so that it begins to manifest in your life, marriage, or relationship. My husband is my best friend. He is my best friend over any friend that I may have and love dearly. My thoughts support this feeling because he is the first person I want to tell about anything that happens in my life, good or bad. I enjoy spending time with him, and he makes me laugh endlessly when we are together. I trust him as a friend to hold all my secrets and to not judge me for any of it. I have trained my mind to never have negative thoughts about our friendship. Each thought that I deposit daily is a thought that brings life to our friendship and our marriage. To create this type of friendship for yourself, you must create the thoughts that align with the friendship that you desire, even if that is not your current reality.

Having an abundant friendship must be driven by your thoughts but supported by your actions. You must take the time to cultivate this friendship by spending time together as friends doing things that you both enjoy doing together. Many times, we find couples that experience infidelity, typically experience it because their spouses begin to create friendships with others that bring them to a place or romantic feelings as well. The same energy you could spend with someone else, you should try to only spend that time and energy with your spouse or significant other. Friendship is a sure way to experience an abundant life together. There is great happiness in finding someone whom you can grow with and learn with together. When you take the time to cultivate an abundant friendship in your marriage or relationship, you lay the foundation for an abundant life of love and friendship to build on. Take the time to think about the thoughts you are having about your spouse or significant other. Do you see them as a friend to you? Would you like to strengthen your friendship with them? If you desire to do so, you must begin with your thoughts. Begin to visualize your spouse as your best friend and picture doing things together that would bring you closer together as friends. You have the power to live abundantly with the power of your thoughts.

An Abundance of Effective Communication

Lastly, an abundant life in marriage or relationships must be fed by an abundance of effective communication. Those that seek to live abundantly in their marriage or relationship, aggressively work at communicating effectively. They make it a part of their everyday life to ensure that communication flows freely and easily between them. Your ability to communicate begins with your thoughts. So many times, we have coached couples that have said that their communication was terrible, did not exist, or was very difficult to have. For these couples, what they said was the truth, but a truth only created by the thoughts that they had about their inability to communicate. My husband and I have excellent communication between us now, but that was not always the case. While we typically communicated well, we had to learn some techniques that assisted us in communicating effectively. If you choose to have an abundance in effective communication, you must first believe that you have a marriage or relationship that communicates well. You must take the time to do the necessary work in communicating better with each other like expressing yourself effectively, listening actively and controlling your emotions. In our first book "Married by God: God's Blue Print to a Successful Marriage", we discussed communication and what it takes to communicate effectively. Here, we would like your focus to be around the thoughts that you are having concerning your ability to communicate.

No one can have an abundant life together unless they can communicate along the way. When you begin to think about your communication in a positive way, even if it hasn't reached that level yet, you begin to set the atmosphere for the change that you desire to see. Anytime you think negatively about something, your responses to that thing will be negative. But when you flood your mind with positive thoughts about something, you will typically think and respond positively when faced with the things you thought about. Thus, if you generate thoughts of effective, loving communication between you and your spouse or significant other, you will begin to communicate in that manner because your thoughts drive you to a place of action. For example, have you ever had someone that you know who had the worst attitude ever? Every time you encountered this person they were negative and mean. Every time you thought of this person, you only saw a negative outcome from an encounter with them. Although this person may have been negative, your thoughts about them also helped to shape the overall experience that you had with them. Because you could only think of the experience being a negative one, that was what the encounter became. You have the power to change anything in your life that is undesirable by simply changing your thoughts about it and believing the change has already occurred. Abundance in effective communication will allow you to experience an abundant marriage or relationship. Take the time out now to change the thoughts that you have concerning communication in your marriage or relationship from what you are experiencing today to what you desire. Abundance is only a thought away.

Chapter Seventeen
Think Like One, Act Like One, Build Like Two

To experience the life that you desire in your marriage or relationship, you must learn to think like one, act like one and build like two. The Word of God says "how can two walk together unless they agree". To truly think it strong, you must get on the same page. You must get to a place of mutual understanding and vision about what you desire to create in your marriage or relationship together. When the vision of two is found in a joint vision, creative power can manifest. You must begin to converse daily with each other to keep each other on the same creative wave and pattern of thought. The more you share the thoughts that you are having daily with each other, the more you can align your thoughts to ensure that what you both are thinking is creating what you both desire to see within your marriage or relationship. There is nothing more powerful than building together. When two people are taking the time to build, you get things done faster, smoother, and you can catch errors that may be made along the way. In a marriage or relationship, the sure way to be successful is to build a beautiful Godly creation together by building unified Godly thoughts.

My husband and I stand back from our marriage in amazement sometimes at what we have built together. We have built a beautiful, loving life together, wrapped in friendship, love, joy, peace, and understanding. When we look at the beautiful, intelligent, and kind four boys that we created, we can do nothing but smile and feel grateful for what we have. Our life is a full representation of what our thoughts first manifested for us in our minds before it ever became a reality. We make a conscious effort to ensure that our thoughts are in alignment with each other and with what we have both expressed manifesting in our life and in our marriage. You have the power to do the same. Once you begin to effectively control and monitor your thoughts, begin to share them with your spouse or significant other, to stay aligned with each other. Take the time to create affirmations together that you desire to see in your marriage or relationship and schedule some time to affirm them daily in your lives together. Utilize the affirmation journals together and work to create the marriage or relationship that you desire. Hold each other accountable in creating beautiful thoughts for your marriage or relationship, and jot them down in your journal. For those that may be completing this book alone, do not fret for the benefits are just as great for you. Anyone that renews their mind takes their life to another level. By controlling your thoughts, you will begin to see an individual change within your marriage or relationship that should soon bring a corporate change as well.

While the phrase "think like one, act like one, build like two" may seem simple enough, it is a tricky thing to do unless you have two willing people committed to transforming their marriage or relationship. To think like one, you must take the time to share your thoughts with each other. As you share your thoughts, you can begin to see if your thoughts about life and love are closely aligned or greatly apart. As you begin to discuss your thoughts, begin to create a visual of what you both desire in your life, marriage, or relationship. What do you want to experience together? What thoughts will help you all create these experiences? Thinking like one does not mean that you don't have your own mind or that your thoughts become their thoughts. It simply means that you both are aligned with creating thoughts that support the life you desire to create together. When you successfully align your thoughts, your actions begin to align as well, as you create the life you desire. If a life full of love is something that you both have numerous thoughts about, your actions should validate these thoughts in your life. You should both act lovingly towards each other daily with little effort because this is what you desire to see, and what your thoughts are creating in your life. Before anything is ever built, the thought about it must be made. You must visualize the house before the house is ever built. Once you visualize the house, you write down those visualizations or thoughts into what is called a blueprint. Once the blueprint is designed, the action begins with getting the necessary tools and material to build. This is what your marriage or relationship must represent to reach the building phase together. As you create the marriage or relationship that you desire, take the time to always communicate your thoughts with each other to ensure that what you are building is the same. If you both desire the best and create thoughts about having the best, then the best should be what you experience in life. You have the power to create that which you desire.

Keep Unhealthy, Unhelpful People Out of Your Business

To think like one, act like one and build like two, you must be careful of whom you allow into your marital or relational circle. In Psalm 1:1-3 it says, *"Blessed is the man who walks not in the counsel of the ungodly, nor stands in the way of sinners, nor sits in the seat of the scornful; but his delight is in the law of the Lord, and on His law, he meditates day and night. He is like a tree planted by streams of water that yields its fruit in its season, and its leaf does not wither. In all that he does, he prospers."* It is important to note as stated earlier in this book, that you must guard yourself from the thoughts of others. As you work to build the marriage or relationship that you desire, you must be careful not to walk in the counsel of the ungodly. Simply meaning to not take advice or counsel from someone whose thoughts do not align with your thoughts, especially when you are connected to God in your thinking. Since you have taken the time to renew your mind, it is not wise to seek counsel or advice from someone whose mind is still bound and conformed to the world. Accepting their way of thinking will only have you going back to experience a life of lack, worry, mediocrity, and limitation.

As you become one in your marriage or relationship, find others who have been awakened to who they are in God and the power they have in creating the lives that they desire through their thoughts. Spend time with those who guard their thoughts carefully and who also watch the words that they speak. Those who guard their thoughts carefully ensure that their words align with the thoughts that they have about themselves and others. It is important to have people around you that can support your thoughts and encourage your way of thinking as you renew your mind. Renewing your mind will have you in a position where you must make a choice about moving beyond old friends or family with limited mindsets. While you may always love them, you will have to create space between you, so that your old mindset won't fight against your new mindset. To successfully renew your mind, the old mindset must die to the new. As we have progressed in renewing our minds, we have had to leave many people behind that we love, to experience the abundant life that we desired. Those people were not evil or bad people. They were just limited in their thoughts and could not support the vision of where we saw ourselves and our marriage. You must be careful not to let anyone or anything come between the process of renewing your mind and creating the marriage or relationship that you desire. Focus on what you desire and keep working towards becoming that together.

Chapter Eighteen
No Limits

By now, our hope and prayer is that a fire has ignited within you. A fire that is driven now by an abundance of Godly powerful thoughts that are beginning to shape and create the marriage or relationship that you have always desired. Our prayer is that this book has taken your focus away from only an outward God and refocused your mind and thoughts to the powerful God that resides within you. You have the power to experience the marriage or relationship that you desire, and you hold that power in your mind. With your thoughts, there are no limits to the life you can create and experience. There are no limits but the limits that you place on yourself by your belief or lack thereof. In *Mark 11:23 it says, "Truly I tell you, if anyone says to this mountain, 'Go, throw yourself into the sea,' and does not doubt in their heart but believes that what they say will happen, it will be done for them."* This is what thinking it strong is all about. Believing what many say is impossible and being able to experience it. Your thoughts and beliefs have a mountain moving power. No matter what you may be facing right now in your marriage or relationship, you can overcome it with your thoughts. Your current reality is not your reality for life. You must only believe in the power of God within you. Connect yourself to God through aligning yourself with Godly thoughts and faith. When you begin to embrace your power, more power is released to you to create more of what you believe and desire to see in your life, as well as your marriage or relationship.

This book has been a journey for us in our limitless belief in God and the power of God within us. We know that this book will transform millions of marriages and relationships around the world because our thoughts have already created that reality within our world. We believe that everyone that encounters this book will not leave the same unless they truly desire to. As we reflect on our marriage, we realize the underutilized power of God that was within the both of us. While our early years of marriage were altogether good, we missed out on creating the life we both desired together because we sought only an external understanding of God and never really connected with the God within us. After realizing this limitless gift left to us to embrace and use, we have been able to create a life that many only dreams of. You have the power to do the same. Your marriage or relationship is only as limited as your thoughts. John 14:26 says, *"But the Advocate, the Holy Spirit, whom the Father will send in my name, will teach you all things and will remind you of everything I have said to you."* God has left an advocate within us all to assist us in creating the life we desire. This advocate resides in the hearts and minds of us all. We must only learn how to tap into the creative mind of the advocate to begin to experience a life of abundance. You must remember that you are created in the image and likeness of God. That image and likeness are not just physical, but also mental. It holds the power to create that which you believe in for your life. Your marriage or relationship is only a reflection of your thoughts and beliefs. If you are struggling today in it, your thoughts are the blueprint to that creation. If you are faring well in your marriage or relationship, your thoughts are also responsible for that. Everything that we experience in life is derived from our thoughts.

You Set the Limit

In God, you set the limit to what you can have in this life by your thoughts and your belief. Many people will teach you that life is limited, and you will only have what God wants you to have. God wants you to have abundance. This abundance is not found in some things but in all things. This abundance that God wants you to have is an abundance of life. Stop placing limits on yourself and blaming God and others for those limits. If you want to have all that you believe you deserve, you must first work to renew your mind. Renewing your mind is simply renewing the thoughts that you have about everything. **Your previous relationships do not have to be the road map that you follow for future ones.** The lack of marital success in your family or with friends does not have to become the life that you experience as well. Your thoughts are what you create with. If the thought does not serve what you desire to create, then dismiss the thought from your mind and replace it with thoughts that paint the right picture.

There is nothing super special about the relationship that Ronald and I share except the thoughts that we have about it. We are both normal human beings who decided to believe that we could have what God said we could have, and began on this journey of mind renewal. Our love is not a love different from what anyone else can or has experienced. We say this to get you to truly understand that it is not impossible to experience a healthy, joyful, loving, and abundant marriage or relationship. It is not hard to create this wonderful life no more than it is to create a life that you despise. The same energy will go into both. You must only decide which one you choose to have and create the thoughts that support that life, marriage, or relationship. You must remember that you are a limitless being because God is a limitless God. All things are possible within him, and that possibility is inclusive of experiencing a healthy and abundant marriage or relationship.

We believe that your willingness to read this book and renew your mind will begin to create no limits and no boundaries in the marriage or relationship that you desire. Most people never truly sit and write out what they desire to have in their marriage or relationship. Even those that do, may write superficial characteristics down and quickly begin to forget about them later. It becomes just another list in their cabinet. If you desire to truly create an abundant marriage or relationship, you must write your vision down in your everyday thoughts. Feed yourself these thoughts of an abundant marriage or relationship each day. Breathe it like air and visualize it for yourself. Begin to feel the joy you have being in a healthy marriage or relationship and create feelings of gratitude around it. You must first experience all that you desire to manifest in your mind in a very real manner before it is created. Again, this may seem foolish to some, and those are the ones that have not learned to take the limits off of their lives and create with their thoughts. Do not let others discourage you from creating what God has released for you to have. They may not see it manifesting in the natural for you right now, but it has already manifested in the spiritual for you. You must keep your mind on the things of God and on the things that you are trying to manifest in your life.

Get in The Driver's Seat

By now, we believe that you no longer have a desire to let life pass you by and to let life dictate your experiences while here on earth. God gave you power over your own life. He gave you power over your own thoughts and over your own mind. You must do the work to take this power back and begin to utilize it in a way that pushes you forward to living and experiencing the life you desire. **Your marriage or relationship is as good or great as you can visualize it to be. You are in control of your thoughts, and that puts you in the driver's seat of your life. You are a co-creator with God in experiencing all that He has for you to experience.** You must only renew your mind and believe in the thoughts that begin to generate from this renewal.

No matter what your religious beliefs are, there is a power within you to create your reality. There is a God power connected to your thoughts, that you can connect to and transform your current life and circumstances. You must only think it strong for it to be so. It begins with every thought that you allow to take residence in your mind and spring up in your heart. As you take back control of your life, you must take captive every thought that counters the abundant thoughts that are connected to God. You cannot fall asleep in the driver's seat, and you must know where you are going to create the marriage or relationship that you desire. Do not seek to replicate someone else's marriage or relationship. **There is no creative power in copying others.** Instead, take some time to imagine what you desire. What would make you the most joyful and happy to experience in a marriage or relationship should be the beginning of your design. Only you know what will bring you joy in this life, so don't seek the opinions of others in creating the abundant life that you imagine.

As you renew your mind, enjoy the journey that this mind renewal will take you on. Do not become impatient when you do not quickly manifest all that you have visualized for yourself. Just as it has taken time to reach where you are now with your previous thoughts, it will take time to change your life with these renewed thoughts. Time is not of any significance. Only focus on the thoughts that you are having and ensure that they are aligned with the outcome you desire. Take the time to also focus on being grateful for what you have in the spirit as it manifests in the flesh. Praise God in advance for renewing your mind and allowing you to co-create in changing your life. Keep your faith always, especially when others may try to persuade you to give up or lose hope. Your thoughts only manifest in absolute faith, so ensure that you keep faith in God's ability to transform your life.

Read this book as much as you need, to truly renew your mind. Begin to pay close attention to the thoughts that you are having and the emotions that you feel daily from those thoughts. Your emotions are a mirror of the thoughts that you are having, so pay attention to them as well. Utilize the gift of spinning any negative thoughts that try to come into your mind. Focus on what you desire to see in your marriage and relationship instead of what you do not want to see. Do not get discouraged when you may find yourself thinking back to your old ways. Instead, begin to dismiss those toxic old thoughts and replace them with an abundance of positive, renewed thoughts that lead you to what you desire. You have the power to create an abundant beautiful life inclusive of an abundant beautiful marriage or relationship. Everything begins with a thought, and if you desire a strong, and abundant marriage or relationship, you must first Think It Strong.